Search for Meaning

Essay Series 13

Antonio R. Gualtieri

Search for Meaning

Exploring Religions
of the World

Guernica

Montreal, 1991

To
Wilfred Cantwell Smith
Teacher and Friend
who inspired my search
for personal meanings of traditions

•

Antonio D'Alfonso, publisher-editor
Guernica Editions Inc.
P.O. Box 633, Station N.D.G.
Montreal (Quebec), Canada H4A 3R1

Legal Deposit — Fourth Quarter
National Library of Canada and Bibliothèque nationale du Québec

Canadian Cataloguing in Publication Data

Gualtieri, Antonio R., 1931 –
Search for meaning: exploring religions of the world
(Essay series ; 13)
ISBN 0-920717-61-6

I. Religions. I. Title. II. Series
BL87.G93 1991   291   C91-090230-5

Contents

Acknowledgements

I am happy to thank Leonard Librande and Antonio D'Alfonso for consolidating these lectures from scattered computer disks in various programs — a task that remains inscrutable to me, our daughter Julia for completing a long postponed manuscript, and my wife Peggy for solicitous editing and proof-reading under unconscionable pressure.

Preface

This book surveys the meaning and development of some of the religious traditions of the world. By *development* I mean the historical sources and modifications of the religions. This approach entails, in the first place, acquaintance with the factual data of historical traditions and, secondly, an examination of the antecedent religious and social conditions that come together to make a tradition what it is at any particular point. But our stress does not fall on historical questions of factual material, provenance and alteration.

Our clearest focus, instead, is on questions of *meaning*. We ask the devotees of the various traditions whom we meet in Ronald Eyre's wanderings around the world what the various symbols of their religions mean to them. *Symbol* is used here in a wide sense to mean such things as holy books, creeds, rituals, festivals, communal organizations, sacred persons, moral codes, religious music and ikons. To ask religious practitioners what these things mean to them is tantamount to asking what vision of reality is mediated to them through their participation in the symbolic life of their community. How is their identity created and expressed in the symbols of their traditions?

This involves, for example, asking Buddhists and Christians what understanding of the self is made available to them by their respective doctrines; asking Muslims and Hindus what insights into ultimate reality or God are conveyed by the various rituals of their traditions; enquiring of Jews and Confucians what perspectives on the historical process or on nature are mediated by their social institutions. In short, what does the world look like to those who experience it through the prism of their religious tradition?

It should be clear that this approach assumes a great deal of respect for the religious traditions of humankind. This is not to say that all or any are necessarily true; it does imply, however, that traditions are not treated as antiquarian curiosities but are taken seriously as repositories of alternative paradigms or clues for understanding human existence.

The form and content of these expositions is shaped in part by their connection with the film series, *The Long Search* (British Broadcasting Corporation/Time-Life). Whatever reservations one might have about these films, they retain the enduring virtue of disabusing students of the notion that religion consists primarily of intellectual adherence to beliefs or doctrines. They see before their eyes the complex and varied panoply of religiousness made up of processions and pilgrimages, ritually enacted myths, sacred music, painting, sculpture and architecture, rites of passage from birth to death, agricultural festivals of sowing and harvest, and the personal perplexities and responses of religious participants as they encounter the challenges of the modern world.

I seek to give a critical commentary on the films by drawing attention to what I consider strong points in the presentation, explaining difficult and unfamiliar concepts, expanding the treatment where necessary, and interjecting objections or corrections where I think the interpretation is problematic. These chapters constitute a kind of running commentary on *The Long Search* films in search of religious meaning, though they can also stand alone.

The title *Search for Meaning* is to be understood in two senses corresponding to the two-fold intention of this book. First, it points to religious traditions as the expression of a human impulse to discover and affirm a meaningful world in which to live. Religious persons seek the true nature of ultimacy, humans, history, and nature, in the face of inescapable threats like death and delusion, moral failure and estrangement. Secondly, the title characterizes the study of religion as an empathetic quest to understand the religious devotees' world-and-value views and their efforts to appropriate and live according to them.

Antonio R. Gualtieri
Ottawa, March, 1991.

A Perspective on Hindu Faith

THREE HUNDRED
AND THIRTY MILLION GODS

The first presentation called *Three Hundred and Thirty Million Gods* is devoted to a study of Hindu religious tradition and faith. It conveys dramatically some of the vitality and the complexity of the Hindu tradition and the way of life of Hindu people. We shall move on to consider it momentarily; but, first, a methodological point.

Methodology is a tedious subject for many so I hasten to assure you that I am not going to devote much time to considering it. There was, however, an important point made by Ronald Eyre at the very beginning of the film which merits attention. He said that he was not an authority; he disclaimed any particular expertise in elucidating the meaning of these religious traditions. Rather, he explained, the authorities really are the devotees, the religious persons that he interviews throughout. If one is seeking to grasp what we might call the *personal faith* or the *selfhood* or the *inner orientation* of the devotees of these religious traditions, we have to listen to the participants. Outsiders might be better scholars of the tradition. Outside philologists will undoubtedly know a Sanskrit text better than simple devotees; foreign sociologists will be able to reconstruct a deeper and more accurate understanding of the social conditions which have led to the emergence of particular forms of religious practice. Historians would be better able to chart the historical tributaries that combine to create the complex Hindu religious traditions. But only the devotees themselves can tell us what the tradition means in terms of its fundamental perspectives on life, the meaning of human nature, the reality of God or the worth and value of history and nature. All of these questions of meaning require us to turn to the devotee as the ultimate court of appeal. We cannot go behind the insider, behind the commitments or the way of life of the participant, to try to understand what a tradition means, because the devotee is the final arbiter of religious meaning of that tradition. And now on to the meaning of Hindu tradition.

Plurality of Gods

Even in a brief film of less than an hour we en-countered a perplexing number of Hindu deities. Let us recall who they were. Ronald Eyre met first the elephant-headed god, Ganesh. That was his first encounter with what would certainly strike an out-sider as a bizarre form for the deity. One can imagine how Muslims when they first came into India with their relatively stark and simple monotheism would have been perplexed and moved to righteous religious anger by their encounter with the multiple forms of the Hindu conception of the ultimate. The first one of these multiple divine forms that we noted — Ganesh — is a god whose role it is to remove obstacles.

Thereafter, Mr. Sharma in Banares who was not only a tour-guide but also a pundit, a learned man in the tradition, said that he personally was a devotee of Kali — a fearsome appearing female deity. Mr. Sharma referred to her as the god in her terrific — we might say terrifying — aspect. Kali characteristically is shown with her bloody tongue lolling out, with a necklace of skulls and a girdle of severed arms. This is a form of expression that people not participant in Hindu tradition might have difficulty grasping as a manifestation of the divine.

Later on we met Sarasvati, the goddess of learning. She figured most prominently in the village of Bhith Bhagwanpur in northern Bihar, thirty miles from the Nepalese border, where the major part of the interviews were carried out. The goddess of learning with her emblems of pen, musical instrument and prism, was being venerated by the students at both the boys' and the girls' schools. We also encountered the Lord Shiva. (I am writing these names in a form that comes closest to English pronunciation.)

Our perception of Shiva, however, was not in his person image, but in an abstract representation called a *lingam*. This, you will recall, was really just a column, set inside a kind of bowl. That stubby column, or *lingam*, is an abstract phallic representation of the god Shiva. The bowl that looks something like a large old-fashioned Roman oil lamp is the *yoni* which is an abstract representation of the vagina. Shiva, as we meet him in this film, is made present to his devotees mainly through the abstract, symbolic representation of the lingam.

We were introduced to a truncated goddess called Lakshmi when Ronald Eyre was talking to Mr. Sharma in Banares in the yard of a potter, where little clay images of the gods were manufactured. He picked up — he claims it was not staged but an act of unmerited providence — a little head of Lakshmi that was at their feet in the dirt. Lakshmi, a female god, is a consort of the Lord Vishnu.

Problem of the One and the Many

This catalogue of Hindu deities suffices to allow us to understand the problem that obviously vexed Ronald Eyre throughout his search for the meaning of Hindu tradition. This was his attempt to reconcile the plurality of gods, the multiplicity of divine images, with the sense of there being a single divine principle. It became transparent that this multiplicity of divine forms did not mean a simple polytheism. When he observed Hindu worshippers, most notably the devotees of Shiva who were making offerings into the pit occupied by the lingam, Shiva's abstract phallic symbol, he noted that they did not appear to be worshipping in a way that suggested that Shiva is simply one amongst many gods. Their piety seemed to be focused upon a single deity. This then was the question uppermost in his mind: How are we to reconcile this plurality of divine images, these three hundred and thirty million gods, with the notion of a single principle of sacred ultimacy, with the idea — to put it more simply — of a single god? We will examine some of his attempts.

The Chosen Deity

The first solution we encounter is found in a statement made by Mr. Sharma in Banares. Note the manner in which he said — in response to the question 'Do you worship Ganesh?' — 'Not particularly. I myself am a devotee of Kali.' This suggests a principle which is prominent in Hindu life, the principal of the *ishta devata*, or chosen deity. It is taken for granted that no single form of the deity suffices for the complexity and diversity of human nature. Because human beings are so different one from another, because of their peculiar cultural conditionings (Hindus would probably say in the light of their respective karmas), it is absurd to suppose that a single and uniform image of the divine is adequate to minister to the deep needs and spiritual wants of all persons. Consequently, in this democracy of the sacred, in this system of divine multiplicity, devotees select the divine form which is most compatible with their own nature, the result of karmic determinations from previous lives.

This, then, is one point we must register at the beginning; there is a vast range of forms of the divine and a Hindu selects the form of god which is best adapted to his particular nature and to his special needs.

Qualified Complex Monotheism

There are various other ways in which the multiplicity and diversity of the divine forms is reconciled with the conviction that there is, in reality, a single, unitary divine principle. One way is to adopt what is basically a complex monotheism. One might well question this assertion of monotheism in the face of three hundred and thirty three million gods. In this context, however, monotheism means something somewhat different than might be intended by strict Muslims and Jews or even Christians. Monotheism affirms, in a basic sense, that ultimately there is a single, supreme, personal being who lies at the root of all existence, who is the ultimate power that determines and gives form and character to all things. However, unlike, orthodox Islam or Judaism, the monotheism of the Hindus is, as I intimated, complex. This ultimately sole-subsisting, unitary, personal being, richly manifests itself in myriad forms.

Those devotees of Lord Shiva who, as Ronald Eyre said, seem to be worshipping one god, are, in fact, worshipping only one god, because in their understanding of reality, and in their system of devotion, the one supreme power that lies at the root of being is Lord Shiva.

One might well ask, what about Vishnu in his various incarnations? What about Ganesh, Sarasvati, Lakshmi, Hanuman, and the whole range of other deities? The devotee of Shiva would respond that in his gracious plenitude, Lord Shiva, manifests himself in many other forms. A Shaivite, a devotee of Lord Shiva, in an encounter with a Vaishanava, a devotee of Lord Vishnu, does not have to engage in a polemic, does not have to seek the extirpation of Vaishnava faith. He simply makes a mental adjustment, declaring, in effect, that the Vaishnava worships one of the many forms of the Lord Shiva whom he (the Shaivite) worships directly with the greatest clarity. This strategy of theological tolerance and generosity is extended to a wide range of differing religious practices. All the other deities are, in principle, simply forms in which a gracious supreme lord has manifested himself in order to meet the full range of individual human individual character and needs.

The devotee of Lord Vishnu would say the same thing, *mutatis mutandi*. The Vaishnava would declare that he worships the one true god. It *is* monotheism for ultimately there is only one supreme personal being. However, he would qualify his monotheism by pointing out that Lord Vishnu, in his great grace, has manifested himself to a wide number of people in differing forms. Consequently, the god that he worships, more or less directly, is worshipped indirectly by other peoples in the other forms in which the gracious lord has deigned to manifest himself.

This qualified, complex monotheism is one of the devices by which the many and the one are reconciled in Hindu thought: Hindus believe in one, personal supreme being, who, nevertheless, manifests himself/herself in multiple forms that are accessible to different types of persons.

Spiritual Monism of Advaita Vedanta

There is another way that a reconciliation of a unitary divine principle with a plurality of gods can be effected in Hindu thought. This is not fully developed in the film, but I think is implied here and there.

Let us start by recalling the holy man, the Mahatma as he was called, in the village of Bhith Bhagwanpur. The term *sanyasin* may be translated as a renunciant, that is, one who has withdrawn from the world, from social and economic obligations and familial ties, and set himself single-mindedly to the achievement of relationship with God. We are not told precisely to which of the many branches of Hinduism the Mahatma adhered, but there were hints that, because of his intellectual background, he might be a a follower of a school of philosophy called *advaita vedanta*.

Advaita means literally 'not two'. It is teaching based on the Upanishads, a body of literature composed from around 800 B.C. to perhaps as late as 200 B.C. — though the dates are variously estimated. The Upanishads are considered the last strata or end of the Vedas, a collection of scriptures embodying wisdom, and therefore are called Vedanta, since *vedanta* means the end of the Vedas.

In the analysis of reality proferred by the advaita vedanta, we are introduced to a conception of ultimate reality which is impersonal. The ultimate is not theistic. It is not a personal being such as is worshipped by the Vaishnavas, or Shaivites, or by Muslims, Christians and Jews. The ultimate is conceived as an impersonal, transcendent essence to which no attributes can be given. No predications can be made about the Absolute because it utterly transcends normal human experience. With respect to a personal god one may say, 'The Lord is my shepherd'. 'Lord' is a personal image and 'shepherd' is another, both taken from worldly, personal experience. One can say about a personal god that he loves as a father, or she cares for me like a mother. One can declare a personal god to be judge of the universe or king of all creation. But about the impersonal and utterly transcendent Absolute of the advaita vedanta, one can say nothing that is in any way accurate, since all language has its home base and referents in everyday mundane experience.

The advaita vedanta asserts that this impersonal Absolute — for whom the usual name is Brahman — cannot adequately be talked about but can only be experienced in mystical trance. Nevertheless, the Brahman manifests itself in multiform ways in human history. We have already encountered some of these ways: all the personal gods, for example, are expressions of this impersonal Absolute. As the Mahatma said, the Supreme God or Brahman is the power station and the multitude of personal gods are dependent light bulbs. But the Brahman exfoliates, puts out leaves (to use Heinrich Zimmer's phrase), in myriad other forms. The Brahman manifests itself in nature. That is probably why Hinduism inspires a highly developed sense of the importance of natural places. Hindus delight in going to the river or to the sea to bathe. I and my wife also bathed in the Ganges at Banares at the riverside ghats depicted in the film. The Ganges is widely regarded as a divine reality blessing all she touches. This explains the great congregation of seven million Hindus to bathe in the sacred Ganges waters at Hardwar. My wife and four children and I have made the pilgrimage to Kanya Kumari, the tip of India where the Arabian Sea, the Indian Ocean and the Bay of Bengal converge, making this a very holy place. As is the custom, we waited for the first sliver of the sun to peek above the horizon before going into the sea with hundreds of other pilgrims. There is in Hindu piety an evident feeling for the sanctity of nature, or at least, certain natural locales. In the background is the notion that the Supreme Being manifests itself in nature. The Brahman is that invisible ultimate essence that permeates all things and yet is to be identified with none of them.

To return to our question of the way in which the advaita vedanta reconciles the one and the many: the claim is made that there is one reality, not a personal god, but a transcendent impersonal essence which, nevertheless, manifests itself universally in the world of space and time. These manifestations, however, are ultimately to be understood by the enlightened as only temporary, as distractions, to be transcended after a long spiritual, educative process requiring many rebirths. On attaining enlightenment one knows the Brahman, ultimate reality, directly, without any mediations or any interposing forms.

Images of the Gods

I have referred frequently to images of the god. We can scarcely talk about images without having to wrestle with the interpretation of the concrete, physical images, or as many Hindus call them, *idols*. I was raised to think that an idol was something bad. To say *idol* was to denote a blasphemous substitute for the one and only, real God. To talk about a people having idols meant that they were worshipping false gods rather than the one, true god.

I have been intrigued to hear Hindus refer to these physical images or statues as idols, and I have often wondered if that represents the legacy of the Christian missions or whether I have been raised on an excessively normative understanding of the term *idol.*

Let us consider the status of these images, these statues or idols. In discussion with Mr. Sharma, as they sat in the yard of the clay image factory, the question of the symbolic nature of these images arose. I did wonder whether Ronald Eyre was not leading the discussion unduly. He seemed very anxious to have Mr. Sharma confess that these images were not divine, that they were simply symbols. In any case, Mr. Sharma did tell us that the clay images were a symbol or a pointer to the divine. They also described the images as educational toys, useful for a preliminary and immature period of one's spiritual education, but ultimately to be transcended in a more direct apprehension of god. 'God is not in a hurry,' declared Mr. Sharma.

I want briefly to discuss this notion of the images as being 'mere' symbols. As a counterpoint to Mr. Sharma, let us turn to Professor Shivesh Thakur, the then Surrey University Professor of Philosophy, who spoke with Eyre in the village of Bhith Bhagwanpur. I would say that Professor Thakur had a more usual — not to say right — understanding of the role of these images in Hindu life. He explained that the images are objects in which the god takes — talking of Sarasvati — her seat. The way that some Hindu commentators have put it is that the image is the god, in the god's image form. In other words, those images of Ganesh, Hanuman, Shiva, Vishnu or Krishna, or the various forms of the mother, Durga, Kali, Parvati are not just pointers — not 'mere' symbols — but are places into which the transcendent god can come temporarily to take his or her abode, in order to be accessible to the devotees.

If you come from a Protestant tradition such as mine, or from a Muslim tradition, you might have some difficulty grasping the notion of the transcendent god temporarily taking his abode in an image. And yet those who have a Catholic background might have an analogy which allows them to hook onto the Hindu experience. I want to suggest, to put the matter in a provocative way, that human rituals create the god. To put it less dramatically, human religious rituals actualize the presence of God. In the Roman Catholic ritual of the mass, God is made present to the communicants. The bread is no longer mere bread, the wine no longer simply wine. Rather, in the ritual of the mass, the bread becomes the very body of the Lord Christ, and the wine becomes the very blood of the crucified Saviour. A kind of supernatural activity occurs in the ritual so that what was once merely bread and merely wine becomes the incarnate god — bodily available to nurture the spiritual life of Christians.

Similarly, to transfer the analogy now to the Hindu case, when the rituals are performed in the context of the faith of the devotees, the images do not remain mere clay. Instead, the divine lord is present in them in his image form. The rituals of the faithful serve to breath divine life into the material images. The *pujas* — the offerings of coconuts or plantains, the sprinkling of coloured powders, or *gee* (clarified butter), the water offerings — all of these are being offered to the god who is for the time being present in that image. Professor Shivesh Thakur remarked, in response to Ronald Eyre's characterization of Hindus as possessing disposable gods, that only the material clay is disposable, the god is not. When Sarasvati, for example, has accomplished her mission of being present at the festival of young scholars; when she is finished her work of bestowing grace, illumination and inspiration upon the learning enterprise of the students, then she departs the carefully crafted images. The clay image becomes, in effect, a corpse. It is then quite appropriate for those young people to dump Sarasvati's image in the river, because the god has left the temporary seat she had graciously assumed.

I have attempted to clarify the role that images of the gods have in Hindu piety. My experience is that visitors to India are much confused by the acts of devotion offered to these images. Professor Thakur reminds us that even the simplest person knows that the lump of clay or anthill, that piece of stone or wood, is not simply identical to the god, for they observe that each year images are re-made and destroyed. Nevertheless, the devotee does hold in faith that the god in his or her grace comes to take his or her abode in that material object in order to be available for the spiritual needs and the worship of the devotees.

Feminine Deities

Since we have talked about male and female gods, I should draw to your attention the practice in Hindu tradition of associating male and female deities. This is a practice which has become of great interest to some contemporary North American feminists who wonder if one of the explanations for a perceived oppression of women in western society is the presence in the culture of the West of an almost exclusively male, patriarchal deity. This exclusiveness of the male is softened somewhat in Eastern Orthodox and Catholic traditions by the presence of the Virgin Mary. But the main image of the divine in the West is a masculine father image. It has been suggested that in a culture that has a male figure as its primary focal image of the sacred ultimate, one is inevitably going to get certain ethical spinoffs in the form of masculine ascendancy and feminine subordination.

The Hindu tradition appears to offer a different perspective through the widespread practice of associating feminine consorts with masculine deities. We have noted Lakshmi, the consort of Vishnu. Similarily, Shiva has his feminine partner who appears in many forms. There is Parvati who is benign, but there are also the fearsome female forms like Kali which are associated with Shiva.

The general name for these divine feminine consorts of the masculine god or lord is *shakti*. The shakti of the lord is his creative energy or power. The masculine god himself is frequently understood to be passive, withdrawn. In order to get anything done in the real world there must be a dynamic extension of god into the world, and this is accomplished by his shakti, personified as a feminine power or principle. This is why we find the widespread worship of masculine gods with feminine companions or spouses such as Krishna and Radha, Shiva and Parvati, Vishnu and Lakshmi. In some cases, this androgyny of the sacred takes the form of a hermaphroditic god, as Shiva is sometimes presented. On the left side, there is a full breast and feminine form; on the right, there is a masculine physique. All of this suggests that in Hindu consciousness, at least in some quarters, the sacred, ultimate power is visualized as both masculine and feminine.

Whether this has any social or ethical ramifications, I am uncertain. It is my impression that some people have examined Hindu religious tradition and society expecting to find, hoping to find, as a consequence of the presence of the feminine in the Hindu conception of god, a correlative social order marked by a respectful, even reverential treatment of women. Whether they have found that causal relation in quite that simple form, I remain unclear, but I suspect that the presence of feminine images of the divine is no guarantee of egalitarian relations between the sexes.

Caste

I want now to draw your attention to the notion of caste. According to Hindu tradition, there is a logical structure to the social order. Logical because it is grounded in the very nature of being, grounded in the diversity of human nature. This social structure can be differentiated in a highly formal and abstract way, according to the diversity of human tasks. There is, first of all, the Brahmin or priestly class. These were observed in the film as they came into the village reciting ancient Sanskrit mantras or hymns and performing special ceremonies to ensure a bountiful harvest. According to Hindu teaching, the Brahmins rank as the top class in the social hierarchy.

There is, secondly, the Kshatriya, which is generally translated as the noble or warrior class. It must be understood that these are very formal, social differentiations that are not immediately evident in the kind of work people actually do in society.

Third in rank is the Vaishya, which is the merchant, clerk, and administrative class, sometimes including skilled artisans as well.

Finally, there is the Shudra, the menial caste, whose purpose it is to serve the needs of the preceding three classes. Priests, warriors and merchants are called the 'twice-born', because the members of these social orders have the right to hear the Vedas, in virtue of which they experience a second, spiritual birth. We saw, in the film, a young boy experiencing his second birth or new spiritual status when he was invested with the sacred thread during a type of initiation ritual. The shudras, in contrast, do not hear the sacred Vedas, they do not undergo a ritual of second birth. Their function, ordained by the religious law books, is to serve as menials for the three highest, twice-born classes. Below even the shudras are those who are outside the caste system. They perform religiously polluting jobs, like disposing of corpses, dealing with sanitation, and tanning leather.

This four-fold social order is a kind of ideal; in practice society is not set up in such simple terms. In fact there is a large range of social groups called *jatis* which regulate the life and social relations of people. The caste system, in the general sense of ordained social classes, is still very much alive in many respects in spite of urbanization, industrialization, and democratization. Certainly at the time of marriage, it would be unusual for Hindus to marry someone, as they would say, 'outside their community'.

Caste also regulates vocation and a tendency even today, outside the educated, urban centres, is for people to do the kind of work into which they were born. In other words, one does the kind of work which one's father did, and his father before him. Professor Thakur pointed out that the one thing he did not like about caste was its hereditary nature. He thought it logical that there should be social divisions according to occupations, but he was disturbed by the hereditary character of the social stratification, which meant persons could never decide that they were better suited for a different kind of work and move outside the class into which they were born.

Westerners are often disturbed, irritated, or even aroused to anger by what they, from their external perspective, perceive as unjust, even contemptuous, treatment of others. What often is not understood is that unequal and seemingly unjust social relations are not the result of personal animosity but of an accepted, religiously regulated way of acting towards other social classes. It should be emphasized that the caste system reflects not only a practical division of labour in society, but also a hierarchical social order grounded in judgements of relative spiritual attainments. Though there are dissenting voices, the traditional view prevails that Brahmins are spiritually more evolved than shudras. The film depicts a group of Brahmins at prayer and comments that they have worked their way up the ladder of spiritual progress through a long process of rebirth. Consequently, they are closer to the ultimate spiritual goal of *moksha* or liberation from the weary round of rebirth.

The Doctrine of Karma/Samsara

Caste retains a great deal of force because it has received a particular religious legitimation in the doctrine of *karma*. Karma can be translated as the law of moral determinism. The basic idea is that things unfold in a person's life in a just and logical way according to actions in previous lives. There is a strict law of justice or cause and effect in the realm of moral behaviour. I say strict, but that immediately requires some modification because some personal divine beings, like Krishna, can actually break the bonds of karma. Until such time as god does intervene to free his devotees from the bondage of karma, one can say that karma is the operation of a strict law of justice in the moral realm, analogous to the law of causality in the physical realm. What a person sows, so shall that person reap. Membership in a particular caste is thought to be the consequence of actions done in a previous life. The inescapable effects of these actions is a social placement that is entirely compatible with the actor's character because of what he has made of himself by his decisions, choices, and deeds in previous lives.

The doctrine of karma is thus made more persuasive by being joined with the idea of rebirth (*samsara*). It is evident that the actual condition of persons cannot always be correlated with the quality of their lives. There are those who are scrupulous in keeping the rules (*dharma*) ordained by the religious law books, who nevertheless experience poverty, ill health and social inferiority. Conversely, some who are openly defiant of religious prescriptions and prohibitions that ought to govern their lives enjoy prosperity and social privilege.

But these anomalies do not seriously challenge the doctrine of karma. Karma is maintained by finding the antecedent behaviour (that caused the present status) in an earlier life. There really is no injustice in the operation of the cosmos. Similarily, bad deeds that are not punished, or good deeds not rewarded, in this life are appropriately recompensed in the next life, resulting in a movement up or down in the scale of spiritual being. One might, for example, be born a Brahmin or an insect depending on one's acts in the previous life.

The doctrine of karma/samsara — moral determinism and rebirth — provides a very powerful religious legitimation for hierarchical organization of Hindu society.

Four Paths to Spiritual Liberation

Our search for the meaning of Hindu faith concludes by noting that Hindu tradition recognizes not one but four different paths that lead ultimately to the highest goal of spiritual emancipation from ignorance and the bondage of rebirth. There is, first of all, the path of devotion which is that of the vast majority of Hindus. In the path of devotion one loves and trusts god and receives his or her gracious salvation. Many will have seen a form of this devotional piety transplanted to North America in the Hare Krishna devotees, who worship Lord Krishna as the ultimate personal being of the universe. They hold that just in reciting the name of the Lord Krishna with devotion, love and faith, one is lifted to the highest state of consciousness and freed from the bondage of karma and rebirth.

There is another path which is the way of action, for those who have an activist mentality. The law books of the Hindu tradition lay out duties appropriate for one's station and stage of life (*varnashrama dharma*). By fulfilling these duties, as the Gita teaches, without attachment to the fruit of the action, that is, without regard for results, one can be delivered from the bondage of continued rebirth in this world of pain and distraction from god.

For those who are contemplative by nature, there is a way of knowledge. The way of knowledge entails the adoption of *sannyasa*, the renunciation we noted in the Mahatma, the former lawyer in the village of Bhith Bagwanpur, who would not even talk about his earlier career. His silence was prompted not by shame, but because, now that he had set it aside once and for all, it was irrelevant to talk about it. He was now embarking upon the transcendental quest for God in God's purity and fulness of being. He sought a kind of knowledge which is not information, not the kind of knowledge that is derived from a textbook or communicated in a lecture. It is a knowledge constituted by participating in reality; it is a direct, mystical knowledge of god.

For some, there is a fourth way, the way of yoga, of discipline, usually involving special bodily postures and exercises (*asanas*) and regulated breathing (*pranayama*).

The Hindu tradition is not concerned to promulgate a single system of spiritual deliverance. There is one ultimate reality, variously conceived, but the ways to that one ultimate reality are multiform, according to the individual peculiarities of one's nature. A way of action, for those so inclined; a way of devotion for those who are emotional by temperament, which includes the vast majority of Hindu people; and, for a certain philosophic elite, a way of deliverance through meditation and mystical knowledge.

A Perspective on the Faith of Theravada Buddhists

FOOTPRINTS OF THE BUDDHA

Is Buddhism a Religion?

The question is raised at the beginning of the film whether the definition of religion necessarily requires reference to gods. If we operate with a definition of religion that stipulates that belief in or relation to god, understood as a supreme personal being, is intrinisic to religion, we immediately have some problems with Buddhism because the Theravada Buddhism of Sri Lanka does not, in the final analysis, have such a god as its notion of ultimate reality. If religion entails gods, and further, if Buddhism's principle of ultimacy is not god, then one would have to conclude that Buddhism is not a religion. Some scholars have so concluded, arguing that Buddhism rather than being a religion is instead a moral discipline or a psychological therapy.

The proper solution to this dilemma, I believe, is simply to widen one's definition of religion so that religion is not necessarily correlated with god in the usual sense. The definition that I generally use is as follows. Religion is an activity in which humans participate in an historical tradition, in a way that engenders and expresses their faith or fundamental selfhood. Religion is something that people do; it is an engagement with an historical tradition or a set of symbols like images of the Buddha, the monastic community, the dharma or teaching, and rituals like the shaving of the young boy's head which enacts Siddartha Gautama's Great Renunciation. This participation in an historical tradition occurs in such a committed way that who one is, that is, the worldview or reality-orientation and values that govern one's life, is a consequence of internalizing the messages communicated by the symbols of one's tradition. This is a very wide definition of religion. It encompasses not only traditions like Buddhism but also secular religions like Marxism. A Marxist might take objection to this definition, preferring to view Marxism as a science of history and society. Religionists, like myself, view Marxism as a symbol system or tradition which induces and expresses the faith or selfhood of persons who committedly participate in that tradition, in a way analogous to customary religions like Buddhism and Christianity. Accordingly, even if Theravada Buddhism has no god as its ultimate reality, it is still a religion, in that it meets the criteria of an historical tradition which shapes and manifests the deepest selfhood or identity of the participants.

Decoding Religious Symbols

We were presented with an interesting case study of how both religious life and religion study function when we were taken to Polonarruwa, one of the principle archaeological sites in Sri Lanka with antiquities stretching for miles. It is not, however, a dead site but, rather, a living town built beside a most delightful tank or artificial lake. We were shown some of the great images of the Buddha including a reclining image of the Buddha's *parinirvana* or death and attainment of the fullness of Nirvana.

Ananda Maitreya, the monk with whom Ronald Eyre was engaged in this particular dialogue, gave a lesson on how to read a statue. One looks at the Buddha's eyes and learns control of one's own vision; one looks at the mouth of the Buddha and grasps that life should be lived with one's speech in control. One of the disciplines that makes up the Buddhist eight-fold path is right speech, which means the avoidance of lies and telling the truth. Then we have a glimpse of the Buddha's hand and are told that this symbolises human activity; humans must work for their own salvation.

There are two main ways of understanding human deliverance from plight, sin, death, ignorance and bondage. One way involves self effort, or what a South India image portrays as 'the way of the monkey', for a young monkey must cling to its mother's underbelly as the mother moves through the branches. The other way involves salvation by the power of another. it is called 'the way of the cat'. The image in mind here is that of a mother cat who lifts her kittens by the fur of their necks. The kittens are only required to submit to the providential care and initiative of their mother. There are two contrasting ways of understanding how one gets delivered from the bondage or plight of the human condition. Ananda Maitreya says that in Theravada

Buddhism, by contemplating the hands of the Buddha, one learns that one is responsible for one's own deliverance. Humans must work out their own salavation, and not depend on the supernatural agencies of an outside force or rely on the grace of a being or power beyond themselves.

The chief point here is that the image of the Buddha expresses the *dharma*. Dharma may be translated as truth, or Buddhist teaching about reality and corresponding right practice. The Buddhist dharma or eternal truth is symbolically expressed in the images of the Buddha. We shall see later that not only the Buddha images, but also the narrative of the life of the Buddha, communicate the dharma.

Two Levels of Truth

This idea of the symbolic transmission of truth is not, of course, exclusive to the East. It is an idea which has wide currency in the West through the philosophy of Hegel, which contends that there are two levels of truth. There is truth in its symbolic or representational form, which communicates most readily to the philosophically uninstructed. This is the level of myth, ritual, ikon. Then there is truth at the level of the concept or rational truth, which is accessible only to those who are philosophically qualified. It is essentially the same truth, but truth mediated in two forms. Images or representational forms, stories of incarnate gods, miracles, and vicarious deaths and resurrections — these are the forms in which truth is conveyed at the lower level of popular piety. Then there is truth expressed, in its highest form, philosophically as absolute idea or universal spirit.

This notion of two levels of truth is commonplace in Eastern thought. There are, of course, differences between Eastern and Hegelian perspectives; the higher level of truth in Buddhist thought is not rational and conceptual but intuitive and mystical. Most Indian philosophical schools take for granted that there is one level of truth for the masses, for the philosophically uninstructed devotees, and another level of truth for renunciants, meditators, and spiritual adepts. This allows most Eastern religious systems to encompass both manifestations of truth. It is not necessary to excommunicate those who worship at popular shrines, including the shrine in central Sri Lanka, where the women went to have their spirit possession confirmed by the shrine priest. The monk Maitreya was a little ambiguous when asked for his judgement on that type of religious activity. He said that he was neutral on that question. His precise words were, 'It's not my business'. Nor does it have to be his business in any ultimate sense, because popular religious behaviour like spirit possession is appropriate for people who are at that level of spirituality. In due course, after a long succession of rebirths, according to their karma, that is, according to the deterministic forces which are constituted by their deeds in this life, everyone will eventually evolve to that state where they will be able to penetrate the image and dispense with it because they have grasped truth directly.

The images, not only in Buddhism but in all religious traditions, embody the religious message, the religious truth apprehended by the sages and seers of that tradition. All of the manifold items of the tradition, whether it is doctrines, or ikons, rituals or forms of social organization, are encoded world-views and encoded value systems. The devotee intuitively knows how to decode them; we outsiders have to work with diligence and imagination to penetrate those symbolically mediated messages about reality and the good. What was said about images in the beginning of this film I would take to be a statement about all forms of religious expression. They contain the dharma, that is, religious truth, in indirect or symbolic form. In Buddhism, the highest truth is the result of a radical transformation called enlightenment.

The Three Refuges

After the initial dialogue with Ananda Maitreya Eyre was taken to a Buddhist Sunday School by Dr. Ratnapala who is an anthropologist, closely associated with the work of an intriguing movement in Sri Lanka called *Sarvodya Shrama Dana*. Any students in the sociology of religion, interested in understanding how religious ideology — religious world-views and value systems — impact upon society, shaping social policy and social organization might well investigate this movement. Sarvodya Shrama Dana is a Gandhian movement which has been transplanted from India to Sri Lanka, and is (or was) enjoying significant success, measured in terms of its social impact upon the peoples of Sri Lanka.

When I was in Sri Lanka with my wife in 1981, we spent considerable time with the leader of

Sarvodya Shrama Dana and we were much encouraged by the reconciling force it exercised. Historical events subsequently have rendered ironical Dr. Ratnapala's statement that he enjoyed living in Sri Lanka because of its great tolerance. Many of us who know Sri Lanka, even in a fragmentary way, are deeply grieved by the outbreak of civil disarray, violence and terrorism which have since bloodied the social and political life of Sri Lanka.

In the Buddhist Sunday School we saw children reciting The Three Refuges, or the Three Jewels or Gems.

> *I take refuge in the Buddha,*
> *I take refuge in the Dharma,*
> *I take refuge in the Sangha.*

In the first place this means I find my salvation, I find my liberation, I find truth, reality and goodness in the life of the Buddha. The Buddha in whom one takes refuge is for many only the historical Buddha. The monk Ananda Maitreya would fall in this category. The historical Buddha is a great teacher and a model of the disciplined life that is to be led by a person who is intent on wandering lonely like the rhinoceros until he achieves final awakening or enlightenment. In the lives of many other devotees, however, probably even in Sri Lanka, but certainly in the Mahayana countries of Japan, Korea and China, to take refuge in the Buddha means to find liberation, truth, reality, and value in the eternal, living, divine Buddha. In other words, a kind of apotheosis takes place in Buddhism. The historical Buddha becomes transformed into a supra-mundane being who acts towards human beings in a gracious, redemptive way, not very different, it seems to me, than the way Christians see the eternal, living, resurrected Christ acting upon their lives, to help, to save and lead to eternal life. Taking refuge in the Buddha means for many Buddhists taking refuge not only in the historical Buddha as moral paradigm and way-shower, but also taking refuge in the living, supernatural Buddha being.

It has been argued by some scholars that one of the reasons the Buddha underwent this divinization or transformation from extraordinary human being to divine saviour is because of the refuge. In virtue of their repeating 'I take refuge in the Buddha', people came to think of the Buddha as a present living reality and not just as a human mentor and model from the past. In either case, those seeking nirvana, those wanting to be rescued from unreality, from illusion, from that clinging desire that frustrates human happiness, those seeking release from the wheel of rebirth, must look to the Buddha as the source of truth and spiritual liberation. Buddhists take refuge, in the second place, in the dharma — the Buddhist teaching. The film does not present a systematic statement of Buddhist dharma or doctrine; it is conveyed episodically in response to different interviews. We shall look at these teachings in the context in which they emerge, so I pass now from the refuge of the dharma to the refuge of the sangha.

Here again, the role of the sangha, the monastic order, in the life of Buddhists, is presented in snatches throughout the film. But it is important to realize, from the outset, that the monastic order is central to Buddhist life. In fact, the great Buddhologist Edward Conze says that strictly speaking the members of the sangha are the only true Buddhists. They alone are seriously set upon the way of life — the eight-fold path — that enables the attainment of enlightenment and nirvana. The monks, the true Buddhists, are essential in Buddhist faith because they are the models of how Buddhists should ultimately live their lives. Moreover, gifts to the monks of food, robes and shelter are one of the principal means by which the laity acquire merit, good karma and, hence, a higher birth in the next life on their long journey to the ultimate goal of Nirvana.

Life of the Buddha

The question is put: Who is this Buddha who is the focus of Buddhist life and piety? We are immediately taken in the film to Bodh Gaya, which is in northern India. If you want to go to Bodh Gaya, you normally fly from Calcutta, or possibly from Varanasi. *Bodh* is the root-word meaning enlightenment, found also in the title given to Siddhartha Gautama, sage of the Shakya tribe. He is called the Buddha because he has attained enlightenment. Bodh Gaya is the place of his enlightenment.

A comprehensive study of the prominent places in the life of the Buddha would require us to go back to the stories that antedate even the awakening at Bodh Gaya, to the miraculous annunciation to Maya, his mother at Lumbini. She is transported into a heaven where her flank is pierced by a six-tusked elephant who implants the earthly image of the Buddha-to-be in her womb. The Buddha's mother experiences a supernatural conception, analogous to the conception of Jesus by the Holy Spirit and his birth to the Virgin Mary in Christian tradition. The Buddhist nativity story has other affinities with the Christian one. At the birth of Christ heavenly angels sang glory to god in the highest and on earth peace, goodwill towards men, while the manger was attended by shepherds and wisemen. The Buddhist nativity story has parasols whirling in the air, while showers of blossoms fall from the sky from which sounds heavenly music. The child emerges miraculously from his mother's flank, already with knowledge and with the capacity to walk and to talk since he has gone through long eons of previous lives to arrive at this present birth. Henceforth he will never be born again, because in the present life Siddhartha Gautama will achieve liberation from delusion and craving that keeps persons locked into the cycle of rebirth, and will attain nirvanic bliss.

Immediately upon issuing from his mother's flank, the new born child took seven steps to each of the four points of the compass, thus symbolizing the Buddha's cosmic transcendence. For the Buddha's teaching is not for Buddhists exclusively; it is the truth about reality for all times and for all places. In his first utterance he declared that this was his final birth and that he would accomplish his world-liberating mission.

A renunciant or ascetic makes a prophecy about the destiny of the newborn child. (This will remind some of the prophet Simeon who blessed the infant

Jesus and praised God for allowing him to witness the saviour.) The prediction made about Siddhartha Gautama is that he would be either a great world ruler, an imperial sovereign, or, alternatively, a great world teacher, leading people to liberation. His father, desiring his son to be a sovereign rather than a saviour, decided to keep his son in seclusion in the palace so that he would not be tempted to experiment with spiritual messages. Siddhartha Gautama spent the first twenty-nine years of his life in the palace at Lambini, just on the border of Nepal with India.

The Four Sights

On one cataclysmic occasion, Siddhartha Gautama ventured out of the palace with his courtiers and en route to the distant city of Kapilavastu, they encountered the famous four sights which recur in Buddhist iconography, chiseled on the friezes of stupas or portrayed in paintings or picture books.

The first sight is of an old man walking with a stick. Siddhartha Gautama — perplexed by this novel encounter with decrepitude — is told that this is old age which happens to everyone; it is the ineluctable destiny of human beings. He is astonished that people live their lives in seeming unconcern, failing to grapple with the realities of suffering that confront them, symbolized by old age.

The second is the sight of a sick person, afflicted with black plague of the groin. Siddhartha Gautama is appalled for no sick person had ever been allowed to come within his purview. Again he is astonished and desolate that in the face of an existence characterized by sickness, human beings can carry on with such a cavalier spirit of abandonment.

The third sight is the sight of a corpse being borne to the burning ghat. For the first time, Siddhartha Gautama is introduced to the reality of death. Again, he is assaulted with a sense of utter perplexity that humans engage in vain pursuits instead of grappling with a way of emancipation from these painful conditions, of senescence, sickness and death.

Finally, there is a fourth sight, which is that of a *bikkhu* or monk. This was sixth Century B.C. India, where one of the standard ways to escape the pain and travail of life was the way of the *sannyasin* or renunciant. The encounter with the *bikkhu* or renunciant opens Siddhartha Gautama's eyes to the possibility of liberation. Upon returning to his palace he realizes that he can no longer pursue the frivolous, vain life in which he had been previously engaged, and he decides to follow the path of renunciation. For six years he dedicated himself to a renunciant life until he was on the point of death.

In the museum in Calcutta, there is a black image of Siddartha Gautama with his concave stomach touching his backbone, the ribs projecting, his face grotesque with sunken cheeks and eyes. He is at the point of death from the extremity of the austerities to which he had submitted himself in pursuit of liberation from this vain phenomenal life of old age, sickness, suffering and death. A woman feeds him rice gruel to restore his life and then he rises and announces to the five ascetics who are meditating with him that this is not the way to spiritual liberation. He resolves to adopt a middle path. He had already lived a life at one extreme of self-indulgence and bodily gratification in the palace in Lumbini. Now he had for six years tried a life at the other polarity of extreme asceticism and bodily mortification and found that it too did not lead to truth and liberation. In consequence, he adopts a middle path.

He travels to a deer park just outside Varanasi. There he seats himself under the bodhi tree, the pipal tree of enlightenment, a kind of fig tree, and resolves not to move until enlightenment comes. Buddhist iconography frequently depicts the Buddha-to-be seated in meditation posture with his finger pointing to the ground signifying his resolution to win through to spiritual victory. He meditates and finally the truth comes in upon him. He is lifted into a trance-like state in which he stays for forty-nine days. Gradually, the true nature of reality and the way of life that leads to salvation is disclosed to him. This is not a revelation from the gods: it is a kind of intuitive insight. He is tempted to desist from his meditations by the demon Mara who sees that Siddartha is very close to final truth. Once he does achieve enlightenment and nirvana, Mara — having failed to deflect him from meditation by tempting him with his beautiful daughters — attempts to persuade him that nobody will ever understand it. He is enjoined by Mara to enjoy the supreme bliss of nirvana and not to waste time casting his pearls before swine. That was a genuine temptation of the Buddha. Would that truth, won by him with such difficulty through austerities and meditation, be readily grasped by the masses?

Nevertheless, he resolved to return to the world, to these unenlightened, unliberated masses and preach the truth of reality, the dharma.

The Four Noble Truths and the Marks of Existence

He returned to the five monks that he had earlier abandoned and to them preached the first sermon which is called 'setting in motion the wheel of the dharma'. This sermon enunciates the famous four noble truths. The first is that life is suffering (*dukhka*). The second truth: that the cause of suffering is craving or desire, or clinging (*trishna*), as we heard in the film. The third truth is that there can be a cessation of desire, and, hence, of craving-induced suffering. There is, in other words, the possibility of nirvana, which literally means 'blowing out'. Nirvana means (amongst other things) the blowing out of the fires of desire which keep persons enmeshed in the wheel of rebirth in which they suffer. The fourth noble truth is the way that leads to the attainment of nirvana, and that is the eight-fold path. In his first sermon, the Buddha shares his discovery of the four noble truths.

A brief elaboration on the first truth about suffering follows. Eyre was very anxious to disabuse us of the misconception that to assert the universality of suffering necessarily entails gross unhappiness and long faces. Nor does it mean just physical suffering. He suggested that an appropriate translation of *dukkha* is unsatisfactoriness. Just to live is to be engaged in an existential situation where permanent happiness cannot be found. We are separated from the things that we want and that separation produces unhappiness; conversely, we achieve the things we want and the result is still unhappiness because we fear their loss. Whether we have or don't have, the end result appears to be the same: a general human malaise which is unsatisfactoriness or suffering.

The Buddha penetrates to an answer why this suffering takes place. It is because we desire things. But what is so bad about desiring things? It is because, ultimately, to desire things is to ground our choices, our life projects, on an illusion. In reality, there are no enduring things that we could possibly desire. Why? For in truth everything is in a state of transience, or instability, change, or becoming. This concept is conveyed in the Pali scriptures of the Theravada Buddhism of Sri Lanka by the term *anicca*. This is generally rendered as impermanency or transiency. All things are in a constant state of change, and if you cling you are clinging to nothing. That was just about the last message of the film. Recollect the image of the train and how it wavered in the surreal, golden light? The message is that the train which looks so solid is really a kind of a phantasm — a shimmering, intangible vision. That image is really a paradigm for the whole of life. There is nothing solid, stable and enduring. Therefore to cling to something is to cling to an illusion.

In Ananda Maitreya's phrase, everything is just a mass of vibrations. Whether that is good physics or not, I do not know. But it is a useful image to express this insight into the fundamental instability or changefulness of all things. They are just a collocation of vibrations.

The unfolding analysis is even more intriguing and, for some people, upsetting. Not only are all things unstable, in a constant state of flux; this is also true of persons. There is a tendency to conclude that in spite of change that takes place in things and in ourselves, there is, nevertheless, a permanent enduring ego, as a kind of substratum, beneath all the variation. Have you ever looked at baby photos of yourselves: preschool, first day of school, adolescence, off to university or a first job, the dates, the girlfriends and boyfriends, the relatives at holidays and weddings? We cannot help noting that there have been a lot of changes. Nevertheless, we typically say that beneath the change there is the *I* — an enduring self. But the Buddhist analysis says that all things are in a state of becoming and there is not even an enduring ego.

Desire is based on a doubly compounded illusion. There are no stable solid things, as we have noted, and, moreover, there is no enduring self such as could desire anything. The reason that clinging or desire is illusory and painful according to this Buddhist analysis is because all is transient, not only things, but also the 'self'. In effect, reality is devoid of self.

In sum, the Buddhist analysis of human existence, an analysis which came to the Buddha in that process of enlightenment, is that the marks that characterize phenomenal existence are (1) suffering (2) transiency (3) soullessness, that is, reality is devoid of selves. Those are some elements of the Buddhist insight into reality that came to Siddharta

Gautama when he became the awakened one, the Buddha.

We should attempt to explore briefly the concept of nirvana that, though it occurs in the film, is not spelled out in great length. That is appropriate, in a sense, for nirvana is something about which one cannot speak. It was said that from the perspective of earthly thoughts one cannot think nirvana; from the perspective of nirvana, one cannot think an earthly thought. In other words, there seems to be a radical discontinuity between the way we normally perceive and live our lives, and the reality of nirvana which is seeing things as they really and truly are. Eyre said that it is like a frog trying to tell the tadpole what water is like. Nirvana so transcends our normal way of thinking, feeling, and living that it is difficult and, indeed, ultimately, impossible to talk about it. Yet, because we are students we must presume to talk about the unspeakable.

Buddha was highly reluctant to talk about nirvana. He used the parable of the poisoned arrow to make his point. In effect, he said: What you really have to do is get on with the job of enlightenment, of transformation, with the life project of transcending suffering. You must not waste your time speculating about nirvana. If you are shot with a poisoned arrow, you do not ask yourself which caste was responsible for shooting the arrow, or with what kind of wood the shaft is made or how feathered. You pluck the arrow out and try to get the poison out of your system as quickly as possible. Similarly, instead of discussing the nature of nirvana, embark upon the eight-fold path, the way of moral discipline and meditation that leads to the realization of nirvana.

This reluctance to talk about nirvana is called the silence of the Buddha. From the Buddhist perspective, to talk about nirvana is both a deflection and an impossibility. Our human, earthly language cannot grasp the transcendent reality of nirvana. Nevertheless, as students we try, knowing that our language is merely suggestive and, from a Buddhist perspective, false.

We can say what nirvana is not. We can say that, whatever else nirvana is, it is the absence of suffering. Nirvana is the absence of desire, the transcendence of that craving which keeps us locked into rebirth in a life which is intrinsically unsatisfactory. Nirvana is the abolition of ignorance because underlying our desire is the fact of human ignorance. The reason we desire things is because we are ignorant about the real nature of things. We are ignorant of the three marks of existence. Finally, nirvana is the cessation of the dreary and painful round of *samsara* or rebirth.

Buddhist Understanding of Knowledge

It is clear that the majority of Buddhists do not engage in the kind of meditation whose purpose it is to penetrate to an understanding of the nature of reality, to be delivered from ignorance, and to attain nirvana. When I say 'understanding', I do not of course mean understanding with the top of one's head. It does not mean being able to write down certain terms in one's notebook. That would be regarded as trivial. When we talk of understanding we mean a profound metaphysical and moral vision. Some may want to call it existential knowledge; others mystical knowledge, some others might refer to it as intuitive insight. We must be clear, in any case, that we are not talking here about an abstract, conceptual knowledge, but a profound, life-transforming, inner comprehension about the nature of the real.

Piety of the Laity

The majority of Buddhists clearly don't engage in meditation so as to achieve that kind of insight into the four noble truths, into the marks of existence, to achieve that release and perfect bliss, which is nirvana. That is an undertaking upon which the monks are engaged. The majority of Buddhists instead try to live moral, upright, and devout lives. The Buddhist laity must adhere to the 'five abstentions'. The first is that they must not take life, and that is why many Buddhists are vegetarians, because they desist even from taking the lives of animals. This is the doctrine of *ahimsa*, which later deeply influenced Hinduism and influenced Ghandi and his doctrine of non-violence. The second abstention is that they must not steal. The third is to abstain from the illicit use of sex. The monks must abstain from all sexual expression. The laity must abstain only from wrong uses of sex; that presumably means fornication or adultery or other forms of sex that would be regarded as perversions. The fourth is not to lie and the fifth is not to use intoxicants. The Buddhist laity must follow this basic moral pattern even if they are not going to engage in the rigorous discipline of the monks.

In addition, the laity are concerned to acquire merit which is an important idea in Buddhist lay-life. Merit is attained not only by good moral living, represented by adherence to the five abstentions but also, preeminently, by giving. Since the merit of one's gift depends on the meritoriousness of the recipient, much more merit is acquired by giving to monks. We observed in the film how on a full moon day at the end of the rainy season retreat the laity flock up to the monastery bearing their gifts of cloth, robes, writing materials, umbrellas, begging bowls or any other useful items needed by the monks to make their life comfortable within the bounds of monastic discipline. By acting morally, by going on pilgrim-mages and by giving alms to the monks, the laity are concerned to acquire merit. This means good karma, which entails a good rebirth in the next life.

In 1981, my wife and I joined hundreds of Buddhists in a night time ascent of Buddhapada (also called Adam's Peak) in central Sri Lanka. The name Buddhapada — footprint of the Buddha — derives from a rock on the summit which contains the imprint of the Buddha's foot made just as he ascended into the heavens. We started the trek at about 9:00 or 10:00 o'clock at night to avoid the daytime heat, and walked all night up an agonizingly steep mountain until we came to the shrine on the top shortly before dawn. The pilgrims had assembled atop Buddhapada at the auspicious moment of sunrise to reverence the memory of the Enlightened Way-shower and thereby to achieve merit and good karma.

On another occasion, my wife and I took a ferry from Sri Lanka to Rameshvaram in South India. In order to get on this ship, we, the bourgeois Westerners, slept on the concrete pier all night. (You can fly in about twenty minutes but we had to do it the cheap way!) Early the next morning, we discovered that a privileged class were being ushered on first — no waiting in line like the rest of us. Most were ordinary Sri Lankans but the Sri Lankan government had given them a privileged position. They were pilgrims travelling to India to Bodh Gaya (the site of the Buddha's enlightenment) to Sarnath near Banaras (where the Buddha preached his first sermon), and then to Lumbini (the birthplace of the Buddha) because great merit is achieved by following the footprints of the Buddha.

The Buddhist tradition has a place for both the *sangha*, the monks, and for the laity who do not aspire to nirvana in their present life. They will in due course, when they achieve an appropriate state of spiritual development, seek nirvana. But for the present they are satisfied to go on pilgrimage, to visit the shrines, and to give gifts to the monks respectfully, for the monks are the models of what life should really be. The monks are not regarded as social parasites. Rather, they exercise an important social function by holding before the imagination of people who are not themselves ready to embark on a similar path, the vision of what life should be in order to achieve liberation from suffering, from death, desire, delusion and, ultimately, deliverance from this weary round of rebirth in the perfect bliss of nirvana. The monk has set himself on the disciplined way that leads to nirvana and, as such, is an exemplar and source of hope for the lay masses.

A Perspective on Chinese Tradition

A QUESTION OF BALANCE

Our task now is to explore some aspects of Chinese religious tradition and to penetrate the meaning of that epigramatic and mysterious title, *A Question of Balance*. Ronald Eyre declared at the beginning of this episode that this exposure to Chinese religious tradition radically challenged his western assumptions in a way that no other encounter did. It will be for you to judge whether this sense of radical disjunction is also your reaction to what you have seen and learned of Chinese tradition. It is sobering to realize that one-quarter of the world's population is Chinese: 900 million in mainland China and the rest dispersed mostly in Southeast Asia and Taiwan (the former Formosa).

Taiwan was the focus of Ronald Eyre's search for obvious reasons. It is still difficult to know precisely the extent to which traditional religion lives as a vital force in Chinese society. It is, nevertheless, interesting to note that there is an institute for comparative religion in Peking to which a number of Canadian scholars have gone. To what extent

Chinese religiousness survives beneath the overlay of the Communist regime is difficult to say. My sense is that certain profound religious perspectives in Chinese consciousness and culture have not been extirpated, even by the official anti-Confucius campaign of a few years ago.

Multiple Chinese Traditions

In examining some aspects of Chinese religious tradition and faith, Ronald Eyre was struck immediately by the coexistence in Chinese piety of three distinctive traditions. This strikes Westerners as a curious phenomenon. We tend to think that if you are one thing you cannot be another. We have all been raised to take for granted that if one is a Protestant one cannot be a Catholic; similarly, an Anglican cannot at the same time be a United Church member. We simply assume that a Hindu cannot simultaneously be a Muslim. Yet it appears that the Chinese religious experience contradicts this exclusiveness of religious participation, a premise upon which most Westerners function. We were told that a Chinese can simultaneously be a Confucian, a Taoist, and a Buddhist.

I wish to draw to your attention various points throughout the film in which this particular note was sounded. We are not talking here about a cultural mosaic in which different sub-groups within a heterogeneous society embrace different religions. Rather, we are pointing to the coexistence in the same psyche and in the same society of three different religious traditions. This was evidenced when we were taken to a new temple constructed with contributions of local people. There was a presiding local deity (of whom we got a very quick shot), but we were informed that his priority by no means excluded the images of other divinities. Taoist, Confucian and Buddhist divinities shared the same temple, alongside a local earth deity who represented the popular folk religion. That is by no means a phenomenon found only in China. Hindu temples frequently have a large number of deities. I travelled in Sri Lanka to various centres of the Sarvodya Shrama Dana, a Ghandian movement. Most of the Sarvodya shrine rooms displayed what we might term *religious syncretism*. There would be an image representing the Christian religion — a Catholic sacred heart, a portrait of Luther, or a popular portrayal of Jesus, for example. Alongside this would be a Buddha image, usually in a seated or meditative position. From the vast number of Hindu divinities, a particular image was selected to symbolize Hindu faith. Something would represent Islam; sometimes, an outline of a mosque; other times, a specimen of calligraphy. This Sri Lankan experience illumined the process we have called simultaneous participation in more than one religious tradition by the same person.

The film took us to a kind of shamanistic seance in another Taiwanese community temple where, once again, we observed Confucian, Taoist and Buddhist divinities. There we were also shown a mural of Lao Tzu, a Taoist sage, a Confucian scholar, and a Buddhist monk all engaged in warm discourse. Although they had spent the day in conversation, they had not noticed the passing of time — so interesting and intimate was their conversation. By means of a variety of encounters, we were given insight into the phenomenon of a number of religious traditions coexisting within the womb of the same culture. The description of a phenomenon, however, is one thing; an analysis of its meaning is quite another. One possibility is that a kind of syncretism or fusion of religious traditions is at work.

The explanation I have encountered most frequently is that Chinese experience represents a kind of religious smorgasbord. One selects the particular tradition appropriate to one's circumstances at any particular time in the life cycle. Thus, Huston Smith suggests that in facing the crisis of death the Chinese tend to turn to a Buddhist priest who is regarded as a specialist in dealing with departed souls and directing funerals. (It is, however, useful to keep in mind that what we saw in the film was not a Buddhist funeral but, rather, a Taoist funeral.) When guidance is sought on structuring the family, on proper relations amongst people, or on how a whole society ought to be organized to create a community of cordial reciprocity, then the Confucian tradition is summoned. When the Chinese want to give expression to mystical moments, to a sense of profound depths in nature and unity with all things, or emotional ecstasy, then they would turn to the Taoist tradition and find there the symbols and teachings that respond to those emotional, romantic, and mystical sentiments. On this interpretation, different religious traditions and perspectives are used according to varying needs at different points in life.

Generic Chinese Attitude

Alan Miller and other specialists suggest that something else may be at work here. Beneath the distinctive Buddhist, Taoist, or Confucian teachings, images and symbols, it is argued, there is an underlying Chinese religiousness which has its own unique quality and is, in fact, the dominant religious tradition of Chinese culture. That would not be a totally unfamiliar phenomenon. We, in the West, are accustomed to suggestions that people may participate in the Christian tradition only on a surface level. Their operative or real religion, that is, the set of symbols that truly determines their understanding of the world, their values, and transformative goal, is something else. It has, for example, been argued by Robert Bellah that America possesses a civil religion. Beneath the specific forms of Methodism, Catholicism, Southern Baptist fundamentalism, or Presbyterianism, which are obviously diverse in their symbols and history, there is an underlying, relatively homogeneous, religious tradition called *civil religion*. Civil religion is a fusion of general Judeo-Christian monotheism with strong ingredients of American national sentiment surrounding the pilgrim fathers, the War of Independence, and other formative events of American history like the Civil War. Even good Italian Catholics in the United States refer to the pilgrim fathers as if they were their spiritual fathers. Beneath the overt Catholicism there is an underlying piety or civil religion that is shared by other Americans in different religious denominations.

A similar sort of thing may be going on in Chinese religiousness. Beneath the diverse external forms of Buddhism, Taoism, and Confucianism, there is a spiritual commonality that is the result of a distinctive Chinese way of looking on the world. In response to the question, 'What is this distinctive Chinese way of looking at reality?', the film offers a number of suggestions. It is to be found, first of all, in the *yin* and *yang* symbol with which the film began. One meaning of the yin and yang symbol is that the good life is inspired by an impulse towards harmony. Harmonious relations of the elements of existence, including individuals within their families and within the wider society, is the highest good. The symbol of balance or harmony of complementary elements defines the goal which persons ought to pursue.

A second feature which characterizes Chinese life is an underlying this-worldliness. When we looked at Zen Buddhism (which moved to Japan from China where it was known as *chan* or meditation Buddhism; *zen*, being a Japanese mispronunciation of *chan* which was, in turn, a mispronunciation of the Sanskrit *dhyana*), we saw that a possible explanation for the transmutation of Indian Buddhism into Zen Buddhism was the infusion of the distinctive Chinese perspective of this-worldliness. This new concern with the natural world, and not another transcendental world, is evinced in Zen's fascination for harmony in plant and flower arrangements and in their rock gardens.

To the idea of this-worldliness I want to add the observation that the Chinese outlook is typically utilitarian. It is concerned with how one goes about satisfying fundamental human needs. The three recurring Chinese divinities represented the practical goals of longevity, prosperity, and posterity. That is a fairly good catalogue of what most people appear to hanker after.

The basic Chinese perspective is not only this-worldly (that is, concerned with the harmonious acquisition of the good things of this life personified by the divinities of longevity, prosperity and posterity), but also pragmatic. Their fundamental concerns are social and, in the best sense, material. Beneath Buddhism, Taoism, and Confucianism (though in symbiosis with them) there may well exist this shared this-worldly and utilitarian perspective that constitutes a type of Chinese civil religion.

To summarize, I have explained Ronald Eyre's fascination with the fact that, contrary to most western practice, the Chinese seem quite comfortable with a number of religious traditions at the same time and in the same person. I have looked at some alternative hypotheses for this. One is a sort of therapeutic selectivity. Traditions are selected according to their ability to meet particular needs at certain times of life. I also introduced the theory of a shared Chinese perspective that underlies the external diversity and discloses the simultaneous participation in different traditions to be a surface phenomenon.

Yin and Yang

The yin and yang symbol merits fuller discussion. On one side of the circle is the *yin* (dark, cold, moist, feminine, intuitive) and on the other is the *yang* (bright, hot, dry, masculine, rational). These are viewed as two qualities that exist in all things. All things in nature are a blend of yin and yang in the specific proportions that make them what they are. They acquire their self-definition, their intrinsic nature, according to the degree of yin that is blended with the yang. The harmony or balance of the complementary qualities of yin and yang makes a thing what it is properly in its perfection. If things get out of balance, then an undesirable state of affairs results.

Though the yin/yang symbol is stressed among Taoists, it characterizes many Chinese schools. It may, in fact, be another common element of the general Chinese religious perspective that I described above. Some instances of harmonious, yin/yang thinking were given in the film. Seated at a little cafe table, a Chinese said, 'There is day and night, man and woman, birth and death, summer and winter.' All reality participates in these basic complementary qualities or phases. Life is a constant dynamic in which one phase harmoniously gives way to another. If night is yin, it will give way to the daybreak of yang. Man and woman also exist in dynamic, reciprocal relationship. The western understanding of good and evil, as a conflict dualism which allows no reconciliation, was rejected. Those raised in a Muslim, Jewish, or Christian tradition tend to take it for granted that life is a holy warfare between goodness and evil. There is God who is a law-giver and defines the good. Over against God and his goodness there is the principle of evil. This might be some personified power like the devil, or the source of evil may be found in the human heart. In either case, there is a rebellion against God, the law-giver and definer of the good, which has to be defeated in a final victory of goodness over evil. That is the kind of dualistic moral environment in which most people in this culture have been raised, if they were raised in a religious context at all. This perception of conflict dualism is challenged by Taoists.

There is diversity, of course, in the yin/yang outlook, but it entails complementarity. The diverse elements of reality are not locked in irreconcilable and eternal battle; the yin and the yang complement one another. The secret of a good life is to learn to live in conformity with nature where the yin and yang are harmoniously blended.

In this Chinese perspective, evil is understood as a loss of balance of the inherently complementary qualities that make up existence.

Shamans and Exorcisms

Let us scan some of the film's other vignettes of Chinese tradition. There were religious elements that were clearly shamanistic; for example, the seance at the end. Further evidence of shamanistic practice is to be found in the place that local divinities, spirits, and ghosts take in the popular piety of the Chinese people. One of the principle functions of the gods is to serve as policemen to control ghosts and displeased spirits. If not controlled or placated with sacrifice, these ghosts and spirits bring damage upon the inhabitants of the particular territory over which they rule. Accordingly, shamans who are, in Eliade's phrase, specialists or technicians of the sacred, are called upon to secure the benefits of the good spirits or to deal with the hostility of evil spirits or ghosts. This was evident in the shamanistic seance which employed chair rattling. This involved a master of ceremonies who took down the messages, a principle medium already in a trance, and two others whose job it was to shake the chair at the appropriate moment under spirit guidance or control. In a shamanistic trance, the spirit takes control of the mind of the shaman. Accordingly, the characters that were written out on the table and then deciphered and recorded by the presiding officers were, in reality, communications from the spirit who had taken possession of the shaman. In addition to Buddhism, Taoism, Confucianism, and an underlying Chinese civil religion, we observed a popular animism that relied upon the spiritual specialist, the shaman, to enter the spirit world (or be entered by the spirits) in order to acquire the messages that were necessary for the living. In this episode, the family of the deceased father had unspecified difficulties and needed a communication from the deceased father, which presumably they received.

Another vignette involved the casting of oracle bones. This also is a kind of animistic religious practice which existed in China some 2,000 years before Christ in the Shang period, long before Confucianism or Taoism made their appearance. Oracle bones (which have been found in archaeological diggings) and the kind of divining devices cast by the ladies before the images of the gods provide answers to human problems, according to the arrangement assumed by the oracle bones or divining blocks. This illustrates the coexistence of this kind of popular, animistic, shamanistic piety with the great traditions.

On a number of occasions the point has been made that alongside official, scriptural religion, there often exists a popular piety whose connection with the canonical religion (that is to say, the religion written down in sacred scriptures or doctrines) is very hard to discern. The anthropologist, Robert Redfield, distinguished the *little tradition*, a kind of popular piety and domestic festivals, from the *great tradition* of scriptures, doctrinal elaborations, ethical codes, and official custodians (priests). Some kinds of Catholic piety in Latin America, for example, can only with difficulty be connected with the official Christianity of church councils. In the Chinese community of Taiwan, we encountered another instance of the coexistence of popular folk religion with the religion of the literati.

Confucian Social Order

Since Ronald Eyre had previously dealt with Far Eastern Buddhism, he decided not to exposit Taiwanese Buddhism at any length. He did, however, go in search of Confucianism. His odyssey took him (and us) to a rural area at the time of the spring festival and the ceremony of the remembrance of the dead. This ritual of visiting, sweeping, and refurbishing the graves at springtime illustrated an important Confucian principle, namely, social obligation.

Confucianism stresses a network of reciprocal, social duties usually designated by the term *filial piety*. For Confucius the most horrendous, moral failure was a failure in filial piety. Sons who did not respect and care for their fathers were the most sacrilegious of individuals. There was, however, a reciprocity of relationship. Just as the son owed his father respect, regard and service, even so the father owed his son nurture, care and training. Filial piety is the paradigm for a whole network of social relations or duties.

Others were mentioned in the film: the obligations of rulers and subjects, and the obligations of the living to their ancesters. The model relationships, usually five in number, include the relationships of older brother-younger brother and those of husband and wife. The younger brother is to be subordinate to, and respectful of, his older brother; the older brother, in turn, has the responsibility of caring for and training his younger brother. The wife is to be subordinate, respectful, and serving towards her husband; the husband has a reciprocal obligation of protecting and caring for his wife.

Confucianism, we see, stresses a normative, social pattern. There is a proper way to live one's life; there is a proper order for society. This is spelled out in an elaborate series of *li* (usually translated 'rites of decorum'), so that persons know how to act towards one another. Our western society still has certain patterns of social decorum. Most students treat me with a certain deference — modest, I admit, and perhaps no more than I deserve. They do not do it because of any perceived virtue in me; rather, they have bought into a system which defines how relationships ought to work. They have accepted a normative pattern for the relationship of student and professor. Almost unwittingly we fall into the mold of that particular pattern. They act as students, and I act towards them with the appropriate posture of professor. That behaviour reflects a Confucian outlook where there are proper ways of relating to others that are defined by one's social status — father-son, elder brother-younger brother; husband-wife; ruler-subject; elders- juniors. Appropriate to each social relationship, there is a clearly defined system of behaviour. That is why the Confucian followers went to the tombs of their ancestors (who are still in a sense numbered among the living) to pay them respect by sweeping, refurbishing, and rebuilding their graves.

Taoist Perspectives

There are two principal kinds of Taoism. There is philosophical Taoism, on the one hand, and popular Taoism, on the other. Philosophical Taoism is the Taoism of Lao Tzu, regarded by some as an older contemporary of Confucius who is alleged to have written the *Tao-Te-Ching* (*The Way and Its Power*). Philosophical Taoism was adopted by Chuang Tzu who moved in a more mystical direction. Popular Taoism may be characterized as the Taoism of magical rites.

Magic does not necessarily carry a bad sense. It is a widespread world outlook predicated on the assumption of a microcosmic-macrocosmic relationship between rituals and the world. If certain things are done in ritual, then certain effects are inevitable in the world. Magic, one might say, is a kind of technology. If the prescribed ritual for a particular end is known and applied, then the goal will come about, provided a mistake is not made in the execution of the rite. If abundant crops are desired, then a rain dance or fertility rite is performed. The intrinsic power of a correctly performed ritual dictates corresponding events in nature. The desire to be pregnant may send women to appropriate shrines to participate in rituals which guarantee fecundity. What happens in the ritual will in due course cause corresponding results in nature.

There are illustrations of this magical way of thinking in the Old Testament Hebrew scriptures. The Ba'al worshippers, who inhabited the land when the Israelites invaded, practised rites of sacred prostitution designed to bring about fertility in nature. Through ritualized sexual acts, the devotees of Ba'al and his feminine consort, Astarte, sought to ensure fertility in the fields, flocks, and human families. The Taoist practitioners, in the Taiwanese funeral, exhibit magical expectations in performing their rituals. The tumbling acrobats, for example, enact symbolic descents into the underworld, as in the Orpheus myth. The purpose of the ritual enactment of a message of death and deliverance is to bring about the liberation of the soul of the deceased grandmother and to assure her a safe and tranquil rest. Until she received that symbolic writ of pardon, her soul would not rest in peace.

Alongside this popular, magical tradition, there is a philosophical Taoism which provides a speculative reflection upon the nature of the world. Further, it holds out the possibility of mystical participation in the ultimate reality, called the *Tao*. Tao literally means 'Way' and, typically signified, for Confucius, the moral pattern or normative social standard that allowed the achievement of a harmonious society. For the Taoist sages, Lao Tzu and Chuang Tzu, the Tao became a mysterious, metaphysical principle or transcendent, ultimate reality. The first verse of the *Tao-Te-Ching* declares: 'The Tao which can be named is not the eternal Tao.' In other words, if you can say it, you do not have it. Ultimate reality cannot be known in a logical, verbal way, but only by direct, intuitive participation in the real. Though transcendent in the sense of being beyond normal routine human experience, the Tao is, nevertheless, immanent in the sense that it permeates all things, especially unperverted nature.

One of the aspects of the moral style of philosophical Taoism is *wu wei* — non-action or actionless action. Philosophical Taoism does not enjoin total withdrawal from the world, as in some Indian schools; instead, it teaches that the proper way to act is in a non-striving way. 'Non-action' means: 'Take no action which is contrary to nature, that is unnatural; do not force your behaviour; act in a way that spontaneously conforms to the given nature of things.' The established conventions, so revered by the Confucians, are rejected by the Taoists as artificial human inventions, lacking conformity to the Tao.

The Taoist paradox is that the way to attain is to act in a non-aggressive, non-competitive way. This insight is communicated by the chief symbols of Taoism: an empty bowl holds nothing and, yet, can contain all things. Water is soft, yet wears away the hardest mountain. The feminine is gentle and weak, yet has unique strength. Other prominent images for the nameless Tao and its corresponding ethic of nonaction are the uncarved block, the ravine, the valley, and the new-born babe. By all these images, Lao Tzu seeks to convey the weakness (non-aggressiveness), spontaneity, and simplicity of the sagely life.

Let us close with a passage from the *Tao-Te-Ching* of Lao Tzu, which conveys the meaning of *wu wei* (non-action), which is the human style appropriate to the mysterious and transcendent Tao.

> Be humble and you will remain entire. Be bent and you will remain straight. Be vacant and you will remain full. Be worn and you will remain new. He who has little will receive. He who has much will be embarrassed. Therefore, the sage keeps to the One and becomes the standard for the world. He does not display himself, therefore he shines. The sage does not approve himself, therefore he is noted. He does not praise himself, therefore he has merit. He does not glory in himself, and therefore he excels. And because he does not compete, therefore no one in the world can compete with him. The ancient saying, 'Be humble and you will remain entire', ...can this be regarded as mere empty words? Indeed, he who is empty shall return home entire.

A Perspective on the Faith of Pure Land and Zen Buddhists
THE LAND OF THE DISAPPEARING BUDDHA

One of the titles of the Buddha, Buddha Shakyamuni, refers to the historical Buddha. He was born in princely circumstances, went forth on his pilgrimage of discovery, preached the truth of existence for forty years, died at eighty years of age after a meal of poison mushrooms, and entered upon his parinirvana. *Shakyamuni* means Siddhartha Gautama, the sage of the Shakya tribe. This image of Shakyamuni, the historical Buddha, contrasts with the 'disappearing' Buddha of Japan.

The Pilgrimage of Buddhism

This contrast recurs in various forms throughout the film. On the one hand, there is Hinayana Buddhism — the small raft — or, more precisely, the one school of Hinayana that survives, the Theravada ('the teaching of the elders') tradition which we met in Sri Lanka. On the other hand, there is the Mahayana — the large raft — which is the kind of piety that emerges as Buddhism undertakes its pilgrimage from the land of its birth in India, moves over the mountains into Central Asia, then eastward into China, and eventually into Japan and Korea. There are many different kinds of the 'great raft' Mahayana Buddhism. We are going to look at its Zen and Pure Land manifestations.

Buddhism moved from India into Central Asia and China around the beginning of the Christian era. Buddhism originally migrated through the mountain passes lying to the north of India, though later it also went by sea into China and Java. To grasp the diffusion of Buddhism, one should visualize the Himalaya Mountains spreading for some 1,500 miles across the top of the Indian subcontinent, mainly in what is now Nepal. Buddhism originated in Bihar in the northeastern sector of India. It eventually expanded westward over the mountain passes of the Himalayan and Karakoram ranges and into Central Asia. Thence it moved along the oases that dot the ancient silk route which bypassed the large Taklamakan desert by either a northern or southern route and, meeting to the east of the desert, carried on into China. This process has been referred to as the conquest of China by Buddhism or, alterna-tively, the corruption of Buddhism by China!

Zen Buddhism

Let us look at the first variant which falls within our purview, that is, Zen Buddhism. *Zen* is a Japanese mispronunciation of the Chinese word *chan*, which in turn is a mispronunciation of the Sanskrit word *dhyana*. The English meaning of the Japanese *zen* is literally 'sitting' which signifies meditation. Although Zen can be called the meditation school of

Buddhism, meditation is not restricted to Zen. Meditation is, however, the focal point of Zen discipline that leads to enlightenment or awakening. I found it striking that the word *satori* does not occur anywhere in the film. Normally it would almost be impossible to talk about Zen without talking about satori, which is the sudden enlightenment that is sought after by this school of Buddhism. It is sudden in the sense of its unexpected timing, but not in the sense of its being without preparation, for satori typically occurs only after a long period of meditation.

We were first introduced to Zen, this meditation type of Buddhism, in a Tokyo restaurant. The prosperous owner, in his eighties, displayed an evangelical fervour about Zen and insisted that his employees meditate at least once a month and during occasional crash courses as well. Because Zen is more widely discussed in the West, we must avoid the misconception that it is the predominant form of Buddhism in Japan. We are told that it is one of thirteen principal schools of Buddhism in Japan and by no means the most important or the most populous. It has had, however, an enormous impact in the West.

Origins of Zen

We have referred to the origins of Zen. When we speak of origins, we may have in mind one of two things: 1) the historical origins which we have already glanced at when we traced the diffusion of Buddhist tradition from India into China; or 2) traditional or symbolic origins. Let us note an additional point about the historical origins.

Zen Buddhism strikes most commentators as being quite different from the Buddhism of India, the land of its birth. Buddhism in India, certainly that of Sri Lanka, stresses transcendental reality. Nirvana is a reality that goes beyond this ordinary, routine space-time reality in which we participate — even at this very moment as we read and reflect. This ordinary profane reality is in a constant state of flux, and no enduring happiness can be found in it. Fulfillment, truth and reality are beyond this world of constant change. Absolute, unconditioned pure being, as opposed to the transiency and becoming of this phenomenal world, is alone the source of authentic contentment.

One scholarly supposition is that when Buddhism migrated from India to China it encountered a different world outlook, a different consciousness, that characterized the Chinese. The result of this encounter was a change in the shape and texture of Buddhism. It is commonly said that the Chinese consciousness is preeminently *this-worldly*. Its primary question always has been: how do we arrange the social order in a harmonious way? In contrast, the dominant Indian religious question has been: how do we achieve liberation, *moksha*, from this space-time world? When Buddhism moved from the land of its provenance to China it underwent alteration in response to the different world outlook that characterizes Chinese civilization. It became more this-worldly, more attached to the world of nature, and less concerned with discovering an unconditioned reality that lies beyond this world of *samsara*, this everyday world of rebirth and change. Rather than seeking truth that transcends the world, this new form of Buddhism seeks to find truth within the world.

If we turn now from the question of historical beginnings and developments, as pursued by modern research, to the question of symbolic origin, as this is portrayed within the tradition itself, then we should bring to mind the flower 'sermon' alluded to by Eyre. The Buddha holds up a flower and the disciples await some kind of verbal interpretation. But they receive none. Then one of the disciples smiles and the Buddha realizes that he has understood the truth, namely, that reality is to be directly experienced in the natural — exemplified by the flower.

This is presented as a *koan*. In grasping the purpose of these perplexing riddles, one may instructively recall the episode in which a novice was asked to meditate on the koan: 'Does a dog have the Buddha nature?' The answer was a roaring 'Mu'. This bewildering, irrational response is, in fact, the 'right' answer. The story of the revelatory flower is discussed in a book of koans called *Zen Comments on the Mumonkan*. This comprises comments on selected koans by Master Mumon, in the thirteenth century, which then received a further commentary by another contemporary monk called Shibayama. The koan in question reads as follows:

> Long ago when the World Honoured One was at Mount Grdhrakuta to give a talk, he held up a flower before the assemblage. At this all remained silent. The Venerable Kasho alone broke into a

smile. The World Honoured One said, 'I have the all-pervading True Dharma, incomparable Nir-vana, exquisite teaching of formless form. It does not rely on letters and is transmitted outside scriptures. I now hand it on to Maha Kasho'.

From the internal point of view of a Zen devotee, this particular understanding of the teaching of the Buddha that we call Zen Buddhism has its origins in the Buddha's symbolic communication with the out-stretched flower.

Limitations of Tradition

The transmission, it should also be noted, goes from abbot to novice. 'The true dharma does not rely on letters and is transmitted outside scriptures. I now hand it on to Maha Kasho.' The 'true dharma' or teaching, true insight into reality, leads to the in-comparable truth of nirvana. Its transmission does not depend on 'letters and scriptures' but on the direct interaction between master and truth-seeking apprentice.

One favourite Zen epigram is:'Burn the scriptures and kill the Buddha.' In other words, you see in Zen a rejection, or a severe qualification of the role of tradition, in the process of ultimate transformation. If tradition means a holy book, a system of ritual, a set of authoritative doctrines, then the Zen devotee seeks to transcend these. His response to tradition would be: 'What good is it to count the richness of others?' The attainment of ultimate, saving truth entails personal insight and liberation. Enlighten-ment, or awakening, requires a personal appropria-tion of the truth and not simply a reliance on the riches of others, that is, on the accumulated traditional wisdom of the founders or the community. Consequently, the teaching is transmitted from person to person in such a way as to evoke personal insight on the part of the novice. The transmission is from master to pupil without ritual or scriptures. The first point, in sum, is that Zen qualifies or, more strongly, repudiates the claim of a saving or liberating role for tradition, whether that be understood as scripture, doctrine or ritual.

Limitations of Reason

Zen is also characterized by a repudiataion or, more modestly, a severe qualification of the efficacy of reason. That is not a novel idea. We have noted it in most of the Indian traditions at which we looked. Most are doubtful of the capacity of logic, of human reasoning powers, to achieve the Absolute or to bring about human liberation. In Zen this point is made with enthusiasm.

That is the role of koans, the riddles upon which we saw the monks meditating at the end of the film. The koan serves to disabuse aspirants of confidence in reason. Some of the koans do make a kind of rational sense. Many more, such as, 'What is the sound of one hand clapping?' or 'What was the shape of your face before you were born?' do not. These koans are intended to drive the novice, the aspirant to satori or sudden enlightenment, away from confidence in reason and towards trust in direct experience and intuitive grasp of truth. This transformative strategy does not rely on tradition, nor on reason's capacity. The koan is a kind of pedagogical device to break down reliance upon reason as a means of arriving at ultimate truth of the absolute.

This reservation about reason can be further illumined by reflecting on the sword ritual that we observed. The chief purpose of the sword fight and the archery, as of the martial arts in general, is to bring about a consciousness in which rational, sequential, abstract thinking is transcended in spontaneous action. The purpose of these physical disciplines is to bring about non-reflective action. The adept gets to the point where he does not brood upon the dynamics and the mechanics of how to swing the sword; rather, he does it instinctively. There is, of course, a great deal of preliminary training, but then there comes a point when he no longer reflects: 'I must wind up this way' or 'I must remember to follow through that way' or 'I should remember to shift my weight from my right foot to my left foot.'

Those who are middle level skiers know how artificial skiing can be. As you ski you say to yourself, 'Down, up, down; weight on the outside ski; lean down the valley; articulate the hips into the hill.' The aim, however, is to get to the point where these movements do not need to be thought but are instinctively done. That is what lies behind the Zen martial arts. The intention is to achieve a state of mind where the practitioner does not ponder rationally: 'I ought to draw the bow slowly; now I must control my breathing so that I do not interfere with the release; I must release the cord gently; my eyes must be fixed on the target.'

As long as one functions in this measured, self-conscious way, one has not yet reached that state of consciousness in which sudden enlightenment is possible. The Zen devotee seeks a state of being where the *I* does not shoot the arrow but where *it* shoots. The archer does not hit the target; the target is hit. Things happen spontaneously, without the interposition of the conscious, calculating ego.

Arthur Koestler, in a somewhat sardonic analysis in his book *The Lotus and the Robot*, says this celebrated acting without any discrimination between subject and object, without any conscious, reflective deliberation upon its mechanics, is nothing but conditioned reflex. That is what we expect from professional athletes. Does a great hockey player like a Gretzky know in advance what fakes he is going to put on the goaler, or has he reached that state where *it* shoots? It seems likely that the moves of a top calibre athlete are so conditioned by training as to constitute an instinctive reaction that does not require the intrusion of the abstracting, discriminating mind. In any case, the purpose of the sword fighting is to provide the kind of discipline that leads to spontaneous, non-reflective action. The mentor attests that he can tell by the quality of the blow whether the pupil has put the whole of himself into a single, unreflected act.

Changing Interpretations of the Buddha

Let us resume the question that agitated Ronald Eyre throughout: Where is the Buddha in all this? Generally speaking, among Theravada Buddhists the historical teacher is the Buddha Shakyamuni. In

Zen, the Buddha has become an internal reality. The Buddha has become your true nature, the true nature of all things. That is why the abbot at one point could say the Buddha is in the stick as well. There is an essential *suchness*, *thusness*, or *isness*, that is, a true nature to all things and the Buddha reality is their true nature. Respecting humans, the Buddha nature is one's real, obscured essence which can be realized through *za-zen* — sitting in meditation as did the restaurant employees and the monks. Clearly, there is a striking transformation from the historical Buddha — the man who was born, achieved enlightenment, taught and died — to the metaphysical reality that is the intrinsic nature of all things.

Tranformative Goal in Pure Land

This Zen transmutation of Buddhism is only one of the transformations that has taken place. A second is to be found in Pure Land Buddhism. Let us take account of the differences between the Theravada teaching of Sri Lanka (which I am taking — problematically — to be closer to the original intention of the historical Buddha) and the piety of the Pure Land.

First of all, there is a distinction in their respective ideas of ultimate destiny. The soteriological goal, that is, the aim of salvation or ultimate transformation, differs. In Sri Lankan Buddhism the goal is nirvana, understood as a transcendent, unspeakable state that lies beyond this world of rebirth, suffering, desire, impermanence, ignorance and egoity.

What has become of the soteriological goal in the Pure Land? Although nirvana, as characterized above, may sometimes hover in the background as an ultimate expectation, the effective or operative transformation goal of the devotees of the Pure Land is rebirth into the Pure Land to the west in which dwells Amitabha Buddha or, in Japanese, Amida Buddha. The Pure Land is a marvelous kind of heaven in which the devotees experience great exultation and joy in the presence of the loving Lord, the Amida Buddha. But it is not simply a case of Amida Buddha presiding serenely over his Pure Land to the west; rather, he redemptively draws the devotees to the Pure Land by his love and grace.

Shift in Transformative Means

There seems to be a fundamental distinction among religions. I say 'seems to be' because on closer analysis in some instances the distinction may be more apparent than real. There is a typology of transformation according to whether one conceives of salvation coming by one's own efforts or by the efforts of another. I refer to this as 'auto-salvation' versus 'hetero-salvation'. This fundamental distinction exists at least on the formal, taxonomic level.

It appears that the Buddhism of Sri Lanka formally puts the stress on salvation by oneself. Buddha is only the great teacher, the great way-shower; it is up to individuals to follow the liberating path for themselves. (In my perception, the actual piety of ordinary people is not so simply categorized since it displays a large measure of salvation through the power of external Buddhist agencies.) Similarly in

Zen, the stress falls not on salvation by another but by one's own efforts, by one's own discipline, meditation, and enlightenment about the true nature of things, especially one's own Buddha nature.

In Pure Land Buddhism, in contrast, the stress falls on salvation by another. Salvation is given by the grace of the great Amida Buddha. The process by which grace and salvation are appropriated is calling upon the name of the Lord in faith and devotion. This devotional act is called in Japanese *nembutsu* — a contraction of *namu Amida Butsu*. It might be said that *nembutsu* is a kind of sacrament by which the Lord draws individuals to himself and delivers them from evil and suffering into his paradise or Pure Land to the West.

There were several glimpses of Pure Land Buddhism in *The Long Search* film. First, there was a visit to a Pure Land temple whose presiding priest was related to the Japanese royal family. During the audience, he explained that the temple was a national shrine for the Japanese people. Then we were taken to a shoe store owned and operated by a family who were devotees of the Pure Land. Subsequently, we got a brief glimpse of a modern, radical sect called *Soka Gakkai*, which is a branch of the Nichiren school of Buddhism.

Nichiren was a medieval teacher who stressed, in place of calling upon the name of Amida Buddha, the recitation of a formula of praise to the Lotus Sutra (scripture). He taught the Lotus Sutra contained all truth about reality and, accordingly, was the true object of worship. Hence, by reciting the formula — 'Hail to the true teaching of the Lotus scripture' — one could be saved. Soka Gakkai means 'Value Creating Society'. It is a curious mix of ancient Buddhism with a modern drive for entrepreneurial, material success. Soka Gakkai does not simply want to save souls for some transcendent heaven. It seeks to make its devotees happy, rich and powerful on earth. One can appreciate that it appeals to many moderns both in Japan and abroad. Their temple at the foot of Mount Fuji is reputed to be one of the largest religious structures in the world.

It is important to take note of the changes that have occurred in the movement of Buddhism from India and Sri Lanka to central Asia, China and Japan. The idea of transformation is implicit in the title that Ronald Eyre gives to this episode: *The Land of the Disappearing Buddha*. Eyre is intrigued by a very interesting mutation that has taken place in Buddhist tradition — so much so that he wondered if the Buddha Shakyamuni, the historical Buddha, had not disappeared either in the Pure Land of the Amidists or in the interiority of the Zen devotees. Whereas in the Theravada school of Sri Lanka the Buddha is conceived, typically, as the teacher or way-shower, in Pure Land the Buddha is perceived as a cosmic saviour. Along with this, there is a change in the soteriological goal from transcendent, ineffable nir-vana to the Pure Land or Western Paradise. We also observed how the nature of the Buddha becomes, in Zen, the Buddha reality within.

The Bodhisattva and the Human Ideal

A further difference between the two main branches of Buddhism is to be found in their diverse understandings of the sacred beings called *bodhisattvas*. In Hinayana or Theravada Buddhism, a bodhisattva is someone on the way to becoming a Buddha. He might yet have to go through many more lives, but he is on the way to that perfect enlightenment which will allow him to teach others the way to truth and ultimate happiness. In Mahayana traditions, the bodhisattva becomes a great cosmic saviour who looks compassionately down upon humankind and delivers them by his grace. This represents a transformation in understanding of the type of sacred person who mediates salvation.

A corollary of this change in the means of salvation is the emergence of a different ideal for human beings. If in Theravada tradition (and possibly still in Zen) the goal is to become an *arhant* or 'worthy', that is, someone who has transcended ignorance and desire and attained enlightenment, the goal in the Mahayana schools becomes to emulate a bodhisattva, someone who refuses to enter nirvana for himself until every last blade of grass has been enlightened. This idea of gracious sacrifice for the sake of others is a different orientation which is seen principally in the Pure Land schools which stress personal faith and devotion.

A powerful image of these bodhisattvas, a great celestial pantheon of intercessory beings, was conveyed by the hall of one thousand and one bodhisattvas. Some of these bronze images of bodhisattvas possess multiple arms and hands to show the plenitude of their grace, their willingness to lift humankind out of the morass of pain, ignorance and rebirth into the happiness of the Pure Land.

The transformation from a religion of self-discipline and self-salvation to one of salvation-by-another, that is, through the intermediary of either a great Buddha being like Amida Buddha or through the bodhisattvas, can be seen in the kind of analogy that was used to illumine this Pure Land tradition. When Eyre visited the Japanese woman who kept the shoe store, she said that the love of Amida Buddha could be understood on the analogy of the love of a mother, son or grandmother, except that it was much greater, more extensive, and more profound. That is the kind of language that is used in Christian circles where God is looked upon by the devotees according to the analogy of human love and human caring. Human love is thought to provide some insight, by way of analogy, into the reality and immensity of the Lord's love.

Assault on the Self

The two Buddhisms observed in Japan — Zen and the Pure Land — strike me as being quite different; yet Ronald Eyre says that what they share is more important than the respects in which they differ. 'What they share,' he said, 'is an assault on the separate ego.' The notion (really a delusion) of being a self-subsistent individual, a separate I who stands over against others, the world, and ultimate reality, must be expunged. The purpose that underlies the tea ceremony is to cultivate the awareness of being 'all there', also called *awareness, original experience,* or *suchness.*

In Zen practice one seeks to cultivate an awareness of the real in common things. Nature is viewed as a pure form of reality that is uncorrupted by the artificiality and the distortions of human culture. Zen probably appropriated this view of nature as the purest reflection of ultimate reality from Taoism, one of the Chinese religions that Buddhism encountered when it moved into China.

The tea ceremony is analysed in the following way. Before enlightenment — while one is in a profane, routine state of consciousness — the bowl is a bowl and tea is tea. In the process of achieving enlightenment, one discovers that the bowl is not a bowl and tea is not tea. After enlightenment, after *satori* or sudden awakening, the bowl is again a bowl and tea again is tea. That could, however, be misleading if it were not realized that the bowl is a bowl in a different way than it was before, and tea is tea in a different way than it was before. Enlightened ones have an awareness of things that is quite different from their perception of them in their pre-enlightened state of consciousness. They can now see the depth of things as they really are. To use the language we employed before, they can now see the *suchness* of the cup.

Take, for example, this eyeglass case which I hold before me as I write. In my opinion, it is functional in that it holds eyeglasses, yet not functional enough to prevent breakage if I were to sit on them. Thus, the case is discriminately, pragmatically assessed according to its utility, that is, how well it serves its intended function.

If I were enlightened, how would I see it? I might still know that it is a case for holding glasses. But beyond that, I might have an 'original' experience. I might sense the black vinyl in its particular shape, and in its particular configuration of shadow and light, in a way that would give me a sense of the suchness of the object before me.

The eyeglass case is experienced in a different way: I would be there with it. The subject-object, discriminating, utilitarian, abstracting consciousness would be replaced by a consciousness of undifferentiated oneness. The legacy of enlightenment is an experience of the co-existence of the self with the totality of all things. Zen's soteriological aim is not to transcend this world into another invisible, spiritual realm somewhere beyond this one; rather, it is to awaken to this world as it really is. As we were told in the film, when one awakens to the world as it really is in the Zen perspective, then the boundaries between the self and the not-self evaporate. One is unified with the totality of all things. Normally, in our routine, mundane consciousness I know full well where I stop. I end at a certain point in space that coincides with the limits of my corporeal form. I know that I am teacher and writer and that others are students and readers. This is me, and this is my desk. We are told by Zen devotees that enlightenment is a moment of translucent joy wherein one realizes the unity of oneself with all things. Such language is highly limited because, in fact, there is no longer a 'self'. There is simply the realization of the *being* or *suchness* of all things, so that there is no longer a discrimination between what is self and what is not self. We are told in the film: 'All things are the Buddha and when one wakes one realizes that everything is one.'

The Amidist Pure Land perspective is quite different. Both Zen and Pure Land, as Eyre claims, may share in an assault on separate ego. I find it much more clearly done in the Zen tradition. The Pure Land emphasizes a personal relationship of the devotee to the gracious Lord; such relation presupposes the continuity of a separate self, even though 'lost' in devotional ecstasy. In the Zen perspective, with awakening, one comes to the knowledge that the boundaries that are normally imposed upon our waking consciousness by the unenlightened mind evaporate in that experience of the unity of all that is. To this the name 'emptiness' (*sunyata*) is sometimes given because all things are devoid of the conceptual distinctions that we normally attach to them.

A Perspective on Jewish Tradition
CHOSEN PEOPLE

At the beginning of the film, in a New York street interview with two rather ordinary looking people, we are given a profound clue to the meaning of the Jewish experience and Jewish existence. It is not clear whether the respondents are working men, tradesmen or skilled artisans. In response to the question, 'What is a Jew?', we get the response, 'We are a nation, a people, a tradition with 5,000 years of history'.

Peoplehood and History

Immediately two notes are sounded. One is the note of peoplehood and the second is the note of history. Much of what we will have to say about Jews will be an extrapolation of the sense implicit in those two concepts, namely, the concept of peoplehood or nationhood and the significance of history in the formation of that sense of peoplehood.

The motif of peoplehood recurs throughout, using different forms of theological language. For example, at one point, in an exchange between Ronald Eyre and the violinist of the Amadeus String

Quartet, the idea of 'chosenness' is introduced. Eyre asks the question, 'Are the Jews chosen to be priests?', to which the violinist replies, 'No, not priests, but rather unwilling instruments of God'. Actually, as I shall try to clarify in a moment, these are not really two different answers but different forms of words for the same answer.

The idea of chosenness, of God's election of a people to fulfill his purposes, rather than the selection of individuals, first occurs here. The notion of chosenness of a people also occurs in an exchange between Rabbi Pinchas Pelli and Ronald Eyre, just following morning prayer at the Yeshiva. I suppose that for many, perhaps most, good modern liberals, the notion of election, of God choosing from amongst the vast range of groups within human history a particular group, is somehow offensive. The poet Hilaire Belloc put the matter trenchantly when he quipped, 'How odd of God to choose the Jews'.

The notion of a chosen people is unintelligible to many moderns, and actually offensive to those who have what they deem to be a highly developed sense of universal justice. This problematicalness of the doctrine of election probably provides the background against which Ronald Eyre raises the question.

Rabbi Pelli gives the answer that the Jews were chosen because they responded. Abraham said 'Here I am' when God called upon him, and it is in view of Abraham's response to God's summons that the Jews may be said to be chosen. My own hunch, although I hesitate to second-guess a Rabbi on this question, is that Pelli's is an unusual, perhaps rhetorical way of explaining the matter, which, if it were pursued logically, would cut at the heart of the essential meaning of God's election. Nevertheless, as a way of emphasizing the necessity of free human response it is certainly a useful teaching device.

The notion of peoplehood occurs again in the exchange between Ronald Eyre and Professor Steven Katz. The concept of covenant is introduced, and Professor Katz explains that God originally made a covenant with Abraham, but in a non-decisive way, which was later expanded in the exodus and at Sinai where the law was given to Moses. In these various references to election, covenant, peoplehood, we get initial insight into the meaning of Jewish religious tradition. Let us now try to clarify this Jewish sense of peoplehood.

The Exodus

The sense of peoplehood originates in an interpretation of historical experience. More specifically, the sense of peoplehood is an extrapolation, a deduction, from the experience of the Exodus. The Exodus refers to the liberation of the people of Israel from bondage in Egypt somewhere around the thirteenth century before Christ, a liberation which took them through the wanderings of the Sinai desert and eventually into the promised land. This cluster of events is what we refer to by the term *Exodus*. In the forefront of the exodus experience is the deliverance across the Red Sea, the barrier which appeared to prevent the escape of the people of Israel from the pursuing Egyptian armies. A miraculous parting of the waters of the Red Sea, through Moses' instrumentality, allowed the people of Israel to make an escape between the parted waters of the sea.

This historical event of national liberation — at least, this story that is retained in collective memory as an historical event — acquires a particular interpretation. It is not simply a sociological or political event, nor a gratuitous historical event that might have gone otherwise. Rather, the scriptures interpret it as a miraculous deliverance achieved by God. God reminds the people of Israel when they are about to enter into a Covenant — a special pact or contract with him — at Sinai: 'Remember what I did for you when I bore you on eagle's wings.' The Exodus event, this historical escape from bondage, is interpreted as a divine intervention that achieved the deliverance of the people of Israel.

The Giving of the Law at Sinai

That deliverance is further understood as the initiation of God's covenant with the people of Israel. It is the process by which God chose the Jews to enter into a special relationship with him. But that is not sufficient. There is another historical event which we can symbolize under the notion of Sinai. It is the assembly of the tribes at the mountain in Sinai, where they receive a special disclosure of God's will. That disclosure is God's law or Torah.

Torah, as you learned in the film, is a word susceptible of a number of meanings. Professor Katz suggested it would be best to translate it as teaching. It also stands for the first five books of the Bible, called the *Pentateuch*, which are alleged to be the revelation disclosed to Moses at Mount Sinai. As

Professor Katz put it, there are different interpretations as to precisely what were the dynamics of that revelation. Was it God revealing word-for-word the whole Pentateuch? Alternatively, was it God revealing on tablets the kernel of the Law — the so-called Decalogue — and then inspiring Moses to write the rest? There are various interpretations. But the decisive point is that there occurred a unique disclosure from God — not so much of his nature, though there are also certain implications about God's character — but essentially a disclosure of God's will, his law for Jews and for humankind.

The uniqueness of that revelation can be debated. Elie Wiesel, the celebrated Holocaust researcher and author who is interviewed at various points, said that God revealed himself at Sinai for the first and last time. This is quite an astonishing claim. I doubt that most Jews would want to concur with that statement: I believe that it is mainstream Jewish interpretation to assert that God has revealed himself to the whole of humankind, in all places, in all times, through the disclosure of his general moral law or what is sometimes called the second tablet of the law.

If you imagine the Ten Commandments as they are often shown, the first tablet is conceived as a tablet whose obligations are binding upon Jews; the second tablet which contains the moral prescriptions about killing, lying, stealing, and adultery, is binding not only upon Jews but upon the whole of the human race. Rabbi Pinchas Pelli maintains that all persons who keep the moral law are considered to share in the world to come. On this interpretation,

God did not reveal himself exclusively for the first and last time at Sinai, but in his mercy and compassion disclosed his moral law to the Gentiles, or non-Jews. All who obey this divine moral law are regarded as righteous Gentiles who are restored to fellowship with God.

The point I wish to stress here is that what God discloses at Sinai is fundamentally his law, that is, his proper pattern for Jews and for all human life.

We should bear in mind that the election in the Exodus is not of individuals; it is the initiation of God's relationship with a people. The events at Sinai give additional evidence of God's choosing of a people. The Torah is given to the people as a whole. Then the people are required to come before God and to pledge their obedience collectively. They say, in Exodus 24:7: 'All that the Lord has spoken, we will do and we will be obedient.' That response of the people at Sinai is referred to as the sealing of the Covenant. It is these two events, Exodus and Sinai, that constitute in Jewish interpretation the reality of the Jewish people.

No doubt an empiricist sociologist would have a different explanation, because his orientation rules out transcendent causes. The methodology of the sociologist requires him to look for natural explanations. The moment he starts talking about divine intervention as a cause of phenomena, he will probably find himself looking for another job. That does not mean that a sociologist may never believe in divine action in the world. He well might in his capacity as a person. But when he does his job as a sociologist, he does not rely upon what we might call 'final causes' or 'divine causation' to explain phenomena. His methodology requires him to cast around for naturalistic causes.

I was at a meeting with theologians and historians and I heard historians whom I knew to be devout Christian believers explain their craft. Historians could look for naturalistic causal explanations of events in social factors like class struggles, in economic or climactic factors — that kind of thing. But they could not fall back upon divine explanations for historical events even though they themselves might believe in such. When they did appeal to divine causality, they were functioning not as historians but as human beings with a dimension of faith in their lives.

The explanation from within Jewish tradition of these pivotal events — Exodus and Sinai — is that they are divine deliverance and divine revelation of the Torah in order to constitute a people pecularily related to God. It is a theological explanation of how the Jewish people came into being.

God as Gracious

Though the emphasis in Jewish teaching falls on law and not theology, it would be misleading, as I intimated earlier, to suggest that nothing is revealed of God's character. Elie Wiesel said that one might have thought that at Sinai God would disclose theology, that is, doctrines about his holy character and his soteriological or redemptive program for humankind. Then one might have expected God to reveal certain truths about the ambiguities of human nature, and about Heaven and Hell and the final judgement. Instead, he gives a law. Nevertheless, it would be misleading to think that there are no doctrinal assumptions implicit in the giving of the law. That has always been insisted upon, I believe, by mainstream Judaism. The giving of the law is an act of grace, of kindness. It is not construed as the imposition of onerous obligations upon the Jews which they would rather have done without. Rather, it is the giving of a law which the Jew delights to do. There is a message of grace buried in the giving of the law.

You will recall from previous discussion that grace means loving kindness bestowed upon someone in need. It is self-giving; it is an act of gracious, caring, loving kindness towards the recipient. The giving of the law discloses to the faithful that God is not only a law-giver, the supreme legislator. It affirms also that he is a gracious being who manifests that kindness in his gift of the law. That should not be a surprise, because already in the Exodus, the deliverance from bondage, we discern intimations of God's inherent character as grace.

I stress this point because there was in the past and probably still lingers in some Christian quarters, the notion that the way to differentiate Christianity from Judaism is by the criterion of grace. Christianity is understood as a religion of grace, that is, a religion in which God mercifully looks upon human beings and sends his son to redeem them. Judaism, in contrast, is a religion of legal righteousness, in which salvation depends upon human obedience to God's ritual and moral demands. The thrust of this interpretation is to imply that there is no divine grace in the Judaic scheme. Commandments are issued by a rather wrathful or at least stern divine legislator, who bestows restoration of relationship only to those who by diligent effort are able to keep these rigorous demands of his law.

That is an interpretation of the contrast between Christianity and Judaism which is highly misleading, for within the Hebrew scriptures, or what Christians call the Old Testament, there are clear indications of a divine being characterized by grace or lovingkindness towards his people. This is evidenced in his election of the Jews in the Exodus deliverance and in his giving of the law at Sinai.

Covenant and Jewish Self-Definition

What about the non-religious Jew, the Jew who does not believe in God? In the film we were told by Elie Wiesel that Jews believe in one God. But there are those who define themselves as Jews who do not believe in God. They do not believe that a supreme personal being delivered the Israelites at the Red Sea and bore them on eagle's wings into the promised land; they do not believe that a personal transcendent being spoke to Moses at Sinai, took him up to the heights and there delivered to him the tablets on which were inscribed his law. Do they by that act of disbelief exclude themselves from membership in the Jewish people? That is something that Jews debate at some length.

The Jewish theologian Will Herberg, for example, declared that the only explanation for Jewish peoplehood and identity is a theological one. The covenant — the pact between God and the people of Israel — is the only possible criterion for what constitutes Jewish existence. Even if a Jew ceases to believe in God, he is still a Jew because God does not rescind his pact. He does not retract his covenant with Israel.

My own sense of the matter, as an outsider, is that belief in God is secondary to the sense of peoplehood in the self-definition of Jews. It is the sense of *ethnos*, of belonging to a people with a shared history that constitutes Jewish identity. For religious Jews this national history is at the same time a sacred history of God's dealings with them.

In Jewish experience and reflection the Exodus plus Sinai yields the Covenant. The experience of divine deliverance, which is really the divine election of a people, reinforced by the bequeathal of his law and the people's pledging to obey it at Sinai, creates that special relationship which is called the covenant. In a normative theological view, it is this covenant with God that constitutes the Jews as a distinctive people.

The significance of this covenant relationship may be clarified by distinguishing it from natural relations between God and people. It is not unusual in religious traditions to have the notion of a special connection between the divine being and the community of devotees. In many cases, it is conceived of as a biological, organic relationship. For example, in Hinduism, there is the notion of the divine being, Purusha, or Primal Man, who is dismembered, and from whose parts society comes into being. From the mouth of Purusha comes the brahmin or priestly class; from his arms comes the Kshatriya or the noble or warrior class; from his two thighs comes the Vaishya or merchant and landowning class; and from his two feet comes the shudra or working class. This Hindu notion also asserts a relationship between the divine being and the devotee, but it is conceived as an organic or biological connection whereas the notion of covenant is predicated on promise, on freedom and purpose. In other words, in the achievement of his purpose God constitutes a servant-people. He elects them in the Exodus; deepens the relationship by giving them his law which they, in turn, pledge to freely obey. Covenant is a kind of relation which stresses freedom in the pursuit of the attainment of a purpose.

Israel's Divine Vocation

We have, so far, said little about God's purpose in making a covenant with Israel. Why did God choose the Jews? The Hebrew scriptures are quite clear on this. It is not because of any superior morality. In fact, the Jews are characterized by their own scriptures as a stiff-necked people. Nor is it because they are particularly beautiful. Other nations were much more beautiful, in the sense of culturally impressive, in the ancient Near East. If one had the chance to choose the ancient Sumerians, Babylonians, Assyrians, Egyptians, Persians or Greeks, who would choose the Jews? If one were looking for merit as the precondition of election, it is unlikely he would choose a rabble of Jewish slaves. And yet they are elected by God. Why? It is because God has a vocation for the Jewish people. When Ronald Eyre asked the Amadeus violinist whether the Jews are to be a nation of priests, the response was: 'No, I am an unwilling instrument of God's will.' But it amounts to the same thing. To be a priest is to be a servant of God. The priest is an intermediary between the divine and the human, an agent who carries out the divine will, who disseminates the knowledge of God and his will to all peoples. This is clearly asserted in the Hebrew scriptures.

When the people of Israel pledge obedience to God at Sinai, they are told by God, you shall be a holy nation. The nation, as a collectivity, assumes a status to be a particular instrument for the holy God. They are to be, as we read in Isaiah 42:6b, 'a light to the nations' or a 'light unto the Gentiles'. In other words, the choosing of the people is not for the enjoyment of special privilege by the Jews, as the oppression and suffering in the biblical history itself and in subsequent history bear eloquent testimony. Rather, it is to be a light to the nations; to be a society charged with receiving a divine disclosure in order to mediate it to other people.

In Exodus 19:6a, we read God's address to the people: 'You shall be a kingdom of priests.' Israel is to be a nation whose task it is to receive a special knowledge of the divine nature and will in order to transmit it to other people. The purpose of the covenant is not for God to play favourites nor to reward some intrinisic worth or merit of the Jews. Rather, God in his own inscrutable wisdom, for reasons opaque to Jews and non-Jews alike, decided to use this collectivity as the instrument of his purpose. The pursuit of that particular goal of trans-mitting divine knowledge and holiness is a mission which entails a large measure of suffering. Yet, in spite of this, the pious Jew, who remains faithful to the theological interpretation of the tradition, insists that the divine vocation is the irrevocable destiny of the Jews.

I have tried so far to show how the notion of peoplehood, so central to Jewish experience, receives its internal justification from events which are retained in memory and narrated in the tradition as events in which God was uniquely at work, to create a people for his special purposes. By his liberation at the Red Sea, the bestowal of his law at Sinai, and his invitation to pledge their obedience to his law, God constituted the Jewish people as a missionary nation.

Jewish Rituals

I want now to return to the film in order to show the importance of ritual. This is a note which we have sounded on various occasions throughout this series. It seems that what is usually fundamental in the religious life is not believing with the head, not the assent of the mind to certain propositions about the divine nature and the divine program of salvation, but rather certain activities which devotees do. These activities are of two kinds. There is ritual activity, which is oriented basically towards God. Then there is moral activity which is what Rabbi Pinchas Pelli called the 'horizontal relationship', that is, directed towards other persons. Most of the religious behaviour which we observed was of the ritual type.

We saw the prayer rituals in Rabbi Pinchas Pelli's home. He put on the prayer shawl with the fringes to remind him of the covenant with God. Its blue stripe represents the sky and aspiration towards holiness. He then strapped the tefillin, the little boxes, to his arm and to his head. These contain texts from the Bible affirming the oneness of God, the reality of the exodus, the service of God and the centrality of people and land. That is a private ritual done in the home. We also witnessed the public ritual in the Yeshiva, where the young men kissed the scroll of the Torah as it was carried in procession.

We have already seen, in other contexts, a number of instances of this type of devotion. We observed Hindus caressing the image of their Gods; Christians stroking and kissing images of the saints; Muslims doing the same to the black stone, or at least its frame set in the Ka'ba in Mecca. This widespread act of tactile devotion including kissing of sacred objects is evidenced in Jewish tradition as the scroll of the law is taken in procession while the devotees touch it and kiss it.

In the northern Indian town of Manali which shelters many Tibetan refugees, my wife and I have witnessed the sacred Buddhist texts taken in procession through the whole village on the Buddha's birthday. The people bow before the lamas and privileged laymen who bear the red cloth-covered bundles of unbound printed leaves, and are touched on the head with the sacred scriptures. This act of devotion to the holy book in some tactile way is a common human phenomenon in responding reverently and gratefully to the communication from the sacred realm to the human.

Shabbat, or the Sabbath ritual, is perhaps the most beautiful and moving in the film. The family gathers and the candles are lit. The Shabbat bread is interpreted, first of all, as a symbol of divine grace. Bread is a gracious gift from the king of the universe who brings bread from the earth. It is interpreted, secondly, as a symbol of the interconnectedness of the human family because the bread that graces the table and that nourishes the body is not the result of the industry of any particular family alone. It is, instead, the culmination of a human chain of activity, beginning with those who plant the seed, then those who gather the grain, mill the flour, bake the dough, and so on. Bread symbolizes the mutual dependency and mutual aid of the human community.

The centrality of the family is stressed very strongly in the Shabbat ritual. I would expect on the basis of the value judgement that is implicit in this ceremony that one would find Jews in the forefront of attempts to react against the erosion of the family, because the Shabbat ritual with its family orientation seems to be so central to Jewish life and piety.

From empathetic scrutiny of these various rituals we may arrive at an important insight. We probably come closest to the reality of religious life when we see and understand, even if only in a fragmentary and partial way, the meaning that the insider, the practitioner, finds in the performance of these rituals. In this brief survey of Jewish experience, we note that a great deal of stress falls upon the things that are done ritually, rather than on things that are believed in the head.

There is a parallel here with Islam where the most important religious category is not the category of theology, if theology means believing certain propositions about God and human nature and revelatory history, and so on; rather, the fundamental category is the category of law. The fundamental intention in Jewish, as in Islamic religiousness, is not orthodoxy, in the usual sense of right belief, but, rather, ortho-praxy, that is to say, right practice or right conduct.

Impact of the Holocaust

The role of the holocaust in Jewish experience needs to be examined. Elie Weisel, the holocaust author, testifies that, after all his research, he cannot claim to understand the motivations of the killers, and not always the consciousness of the victims.

There can scarcely be any doubt that the holocaust has become the central symbol for modern Jewish consciousness. It is largely in response to the holocaust that the drive for the re-creation of Israel, as a political state, has emerged. It is unlikely that the kind of Zionism called political Zionism, whose thrust was not simply to preserve Jewish language and values as in cultural Zionism, nor only to revivify a Jewish sense of relationship to God, as in religious Zionism, would have got off the ground in so short a time in recent history except as a reaction to the holocaust. In the light of the near extermination of West European Jewry at the hands of the Nazis, the claims of political Zionists that the only proper, normative, manifestation of Jewish life is as a nation in its own land with its own political structures, appeared compelling.

The holocaust has been a severe challenge to Jews whose theological task it is to reflect upon the role of God in relation to Jewish existence. A theologian, Richard Rubenstein, in a book called *After Auschwitz* declared that after the holocaust it is impossible to believe in a sovereign God of history like the God of the Bible. The God of the Bible acts in historical events like the Exodus and Sinai. Rubenstein concluded that it is impossible to believe in a God who acts powerfully and providentially in history in the light of the holocaust. One must now say either that God is so weak as to not warrant worship because he could not counteract the demonic evil of the holocaust, or else, assuming that God has power, that he is not the loving being that one had assumed because he allowed the imponderable evil of the holocaust to occur. Rubenstein's position is that, after Auschwitz, it is not credible that one affirm a God who is the lord of history who rules it in a loving and providential way.

The contrary position was advanced by Emile Fackenheim who said that Jews must not give posthumous victories to Hitler. If the Jews were to capitulate to theological cynicism, in which they lamented that it is no longer possible to believe in God, Hitler would have won a double victory. He would have won the victory of the holocaust, the near destruction of European Jewry, and now, in addition, he would win a posthumous victory in which Jews would be alienated from their traditional faith in the living and loving Lord of history. Fackenheim argued that Jews have to somehow find a place even for the holocaust within their traditional belief in God.

The holocaust has seared Jewish consciousness in a way which is sometimes very hard for non-Jews to understand. Many of the developments of the Middle East arising out of the Palestinian/Israeli struggle, which would be unintelligible if one were to apply ordinary criteria of justice, autonomy, and self-determination, can be understood, in part, against the background of the Jewish experience of the holocaust. A perplexing reluctance, even refusal, to accept the prospect of a Palestinian national state as the only historically realistic solution to the competition of two nations for the same piece of land in the Middle East receives a certain psychological intelligibility if one understands what the holocaust, the destruction of the six million, means in Jewish consciousness.

A dominant note in the holocaust mentality is Fackenheim's assertion of an eleventh commandment to the Jews: 'You shall survive.' A failure to survive means the award of a posthumous victory to Hitler.

Jewish-Christian Relations

One last point concerns how we are to understand, theologically, the relation of Christians and Jews. The Christian way to understand it, in the past, was to say that all of the promises that God made to the children of Israel according to the flesh, the descendants of Abraham, have now passed over to the new

Israel which is the Church. From the Christian perspective the continuing Jewish religious tradition is an anomaly. Israel has been superseded by the Church. The divine promise and vocation, the covenant and mission, passed over to the Church with the coming of the Messiah.

But there is another way of understanding the relation which was proposed by the Jewish theologian, Franz Rosensweig. There is, in reality, only one people of God divided into two entities — Israel and the Church — each with a different mission. God's covenant with the Jews requires them to look inward in order to preserve the unity of God. The moment the people of God abandon a kind of collective insulation and move out into the pagan world, there is a danger of polytheism. Consequently, the Jews have laid upon them, as a divine division of labour, an inward looking mission to retain the unity and uniqueness of God's character.

Christians, on the outside of the circle, have a divine mandate to look outward, to bear the name of God to the Gentiles, to all of the peoples of the world. There is one covenant people, but divided into two distinct callings; the Jewish mission inward in the interest of monotheism, and the Christian mission outward in the interest of evangelization. This way of understanding the relation between Christians and Jews has been held by some theologians of both faiths.

My own view, speaking here as a student of religion, is to see the two traditions as two autonomous traditions, each working in its own way, on the basis of its own symbolic life, to mediate meaning and value, transformation or salvation to their respective devotees. Instead of trying to make Jews into crypto-Christians, or Christians into residual Jews, it is more fruitful to view them as two distinct communities, though closely related both historically and conceptually, bearing meaning, value and salvation to their respective participants.

A Perspective on
Roman Catholic Faith

ROME, LEEDS AND THE DESERT

Papal authority

The film begins in St. Peter's Square in Rome. We see the Pope (then Paul VI) borne on a palanquin into St. Peter's Cathedral, down the length of the nave where he takes his position under the baldachino or canopy that covers the large main altar. There he celebrates a high mass with some of the cardinals in attendance. Almost immediately we are introduced to a doctrine of historical importance to Catholic faith and a stumbling block for many Protestants — the doctrine of apostolic succession and papal primacy. The reason the pope is accorded such prominence is because he is understood to be Christ's vicar or deputy on earth. As such, the pope exercises Christ's authority.

The question of authority is fundamental in any interpretation of religion. In the last analysis, if we want to understand the meaning of religious traditions, we have to ask for the authority or grounding of their beliefs, reality-perceptions, orientations on the world, and their values. What vindicates or justifies the particular outlook and value system to which they are committed?

I suppose Christians of any persuasion if pressed on the question of authority for their beliefs and values, their perception of what is true and good, would answer 'Jesus Christ'. This does not, however, entirely answer the question because we are left with the dilemma of trying to ascertain how Christ exercises his authority over human beings at the present time. Here we would find considerable diversity. The Catholic position is that religious norms are established ultimately by the bishop of Rome because Christ, while he was still on earth, bequeathed his authority of teaching and governing to the first bishop of Rome, the Apostle Peter. Peter, the first pope, in turn transmitted that dominical authority to all the successive bishops of Rome.

We heard Mrs. Dryhurst, in her kitchen conversation with Ronald Eyre, declare that locating teaching and governing authority in the pope, the bishop of Rome, is a source both of reassuring certitude and of constant perplexity. One wants to have, she explained, a mature faith wherein the truth is grasped for oneself, not simply accepted on the authority of an external person or institution. And yet there are times, she acknowledged, that one wants to know that there is a final resting place, that there is an ultimate point to which one can turn to find what one ought to believe as the truth about existence, and what one ought to pursue as the true good.

For Roman Catholics the authority for metaphysical or spiritual truth and moral goodness is, in principle, to be found in Christ. But Christ has intended his guidance to be historically available to human beings in a particular way, that is, in the bishop of Rome, the pope. To say that the pope is the seat of authority is not to say that the pope is right in all matters. For Catholics this point is commonplace, but it may not be appreciated by non-Catholics. Hence, it will bear clarification.

The pope speaks authoritatively and infallibly only when he speaks on matters of faith and morals and, moreover, when he speaks ex-cathedra. This means the pope is infallible only when his declarations from the throne of the bishop of Rome are intended to promulgate the truth about Christian faith and the Christian way of life. When he passes opinions about astronomy, biology or astrophysics, his views are not binding. But when he speaks on faith (that is, the understanding of God and persons in the salvation process) or on morals (that is, the good that ought to be pursued), with the intention of setting forth the true interpretation of the Christian revelation for all of the faithful, then he speaks infallibly. It should be noted that the pope is infallible not in his private capacity as a good person nor as a devout priest but, rather, as the vicar or deputy of Christ.

It is only in this restricted way that one can properly speak of the infallibility of the pope who is the proximate authority for Catholic faith — bearing in mind that the ultimate authority is Jesus Christ. That is what we mean by apostolic succession and papal primacy. Christ truly is the sole head of the Church. However, as an act of grace toward humans, he bestowed his authority of interpreting truth and of ruling and guiding the Church to Peter, the first bishop of Rome, who in turn bestowed that authority through the laying on of hands to the successive bishops of Rome. That explains the prominence given to Paul VI and why he is borne high on the palanquin as he enters St. Peter's Cathedral. The applause he receives is because he is the vicar of Christ, the historical presence of the authority of Jesus Christ in the lives of the faithful.

I recall my utter astonishment when I attended an audience with the pope in 1955 while studying in Rome. My wife and I arranged to have an audience with hundreds of other people in a great hall. We were deeply perplexed and anxious as the time drew near for the pope to enter the audience hall. Remember, this was 1955. At that time, Roman Catholics and Protestants understood each other quite differently. We wondered how we should react because undoubtedly all these benighted, papist masses would throw themselves down before the pope in abject subservience when he came in, and we would be left standing out like sore thumbs. To our astonishment, when the pope came in the people broke into cheers of 'Viv' il papa' and applauded loudly. It was like a great secular hero being greeted, like Gaetan Boucher being welcomed back to Canada after winning three Olympic gold medals for speed skating! The prominence given to the pope, however, is due to his being viewed as the historical agency of Christ's guidance and oversight of the Church through the ages since his ascension into heaven.

Expressions of Faith

Since we had major references to the Catholic ritual of the mass at least four times in the film, it is fitting that we seek to grasp its meaning. To do this we shall first examine the general role of ritual in religious life.

I sometimes employ a method in the study of religion which is broadly classed as *phenomenology*. This approach seeks to discern a generic essence within a variety of particular historical manifestations. Let us, accordingly, try to uncover some of the common structures of religious life.

It is commonly said that religious faith finds expression in three principal forms. By *faith* I mean something like this: the inner core of personality that flows from one's fundamental perspectives on reality. This includes those judgments people make about the nature of ultimacy; the true nature of human beings; the meaning of the historical process (that is, the course of collective events in time); and finally, a perspective on the natural world (that is, how they understand and evaluate the natural environment in which they live). These various outlooks or perspectives on reality constitute one dimension of faith.

There must, of course, be profound commitment. Faith is never only a matter of entertaining certain ideas about reality: about gods, humans, history and nature. It entails commitment. If there is no commitment, if there is no gathering up of all the human dimensions of feeling, willing, thinking and striving, and focusing them on the disclosure of what is held to be true, then there is no faith. Having interesting, diverse ideas about existence does not bring about faith. Faith necessarily entails the ingredient of self-consecration to a world-view and, as a corollary of that, the appropriation of a commensurate set of values.

This is a rough definition of faith: faith entails reality-perspectives (that is, ways of looking upon what is truly real), commitment to them, and then resolving to act according to values which are implicit in those reality- perspectives.

The first way faith expresses itself is in thought. By *thought* I mean both myth and doctrine. Myths are stories about gods and their relation to the earth and to human beings. They may, if correctly interpreted, convey a message of reality and a paradigm or model for how humans ought to live. Another intellectual way in which faith finds expression is doctrine, which is more formal, abstract and conceptual than the imaginative stories of myth. Creeds may be regarded as condensed forms or succinct summaries of doctrine, particularly useful for instructing converts, testing faith, or expressing agreement.

The second main way that faith expresses itself is in cult or ritual action. Some students of religion argue that rituals are much more important than creeds or doctrines in the lives of the faithful. I suspect that they are right. The preoccupation with creeds and doctrines — the Thirty-Nine Articles, the Heidelberg Confession, the Westminster Confession, the United Church Basis of Union, and so on — is a rather parochial fixation in the sense that it is largely a western intellectualist concern. If we try to understand religiousness in the context of humankind's global diversity and historical variegation, then I think we would see that what people do in their liturgical or worship actions is much more important in their religious lives than what they think. Most religious participants are not intellectually trained to appreciate a doctrine. Most devotees, however, do take part in the rituals or worship life of their communities.

The third way that religious faith finds expression is in community or fellowship. The social reality of the Church, in all its diversity, is the Christian and Catholic form of this. Creed, cult and community are the principal forms in which faith is expressed, though one ought not to suppose that they exhaust the ways in which faith manifests itself. What is left out of this list is, for example, the rich iconography of religion. One need only recall the Black Madonna of Monserrat. A place might be found for the image of Mary under the category of 'ritual', but it is probably best understood as a separate manifestation. Iconography or image-making is one of the prominent ways in which faith finds expression, as we already noted in both the Hindu and Buddhist traditions. Sacred books or scriptures might be included under 'creed', although I think that that could be misleading. Probably the most important religious expression that has been omitted is the expression of faith in morality.

Morality could be subsumed under 'action', but typically in religious studies 'action' means cultic or ritual action. By *moral* I mean the obligatory ways in which people relate to one another. This is not, let me hasten to add, an exhaustive list. Rather, it is a useful summary of some of the main ways in which faith finds expression in human history.

Sacrament of the Mass

Against this general background of diverse religious expressions of faith, let us focus now on the dominant cultic or ritual expression of Catholic faith, that is, the mass, known also as the eucharist, holy communion, or the sacrament of the bread and wine.

This is a recurrent theme throughout the film. We encountered the mass in the Jesus Room in the Leeds' rowhouse of the Little Brothers of Christ. One of the most moving vignettes of the whole film is the picture of the Dutch brother leading his companions, gathered in an upper room of their rowhouse to celebrate the mass, in prayer. We observed the celebration of the ritual of the bread and the wine once again in central Spain. The Brothers stood round with extended open hands to receive the grace of Christ in the form of bread, while a guitar provided the accompaniment for their singing of hymns. A variant of the mass occurs again in a desert cave. When the brothers go up to the cave for their period of contemplation, they bear in their rucksacks a consecrated host or wafer of unleavened bread.

Ronald Eyre says that in the celebration of the papal mass at St. Peter's, the man who entered as a king then bowed like a servant. Why did Pope Paul VI kneel at the altar? It was because the consecrated host — that round unleavened wafer which the pope held aloft for the devout to venerate — had become, through the miracle of the mass, the body of Christ. When a priest declares in the context of the liturgy 'This is my body', through the operation of a super-natural power that bread indeed becomes the body of Christ to nurture the lives of the faithful. That is why the pope, notwithstanding that he was the vicar or the deputy of Christ on earth, knelt. That is also why the Little Brothers of Christ in Spain, when they went on their retreat to the mountain cave, took with them a consecrated host which had been blessed in the ritual of the mass. The bread had become the body of Christ, that is, the very presence of Christ. Bearing the host with them up to the cave they were, strictly speaking, not alone. Christ, who is in principle available to the faithful at all times and in all places, is present on earth in a special way through the consecrated host.

I remember my youth in Montreal from about the age of twelve on. It was quite a culture shock in those days (1942) for a pious Protestant to go from a southern Ontario town to Quebec where Catholic piety of a certain kind was still highly evident. In Quebec, the faithful removed their hats or bowed their heads as they walked by churches or passed by in overcrowded streetcars. Why? Because Christ was present in the consecrated host on the altar.

That is the kind of piety that is present in the ritual of the mass — a recurring motif throughout the film.

Diversity within the Catholic Church

I want to comment briefly upon the diversity within the Roman Catholic Church. I was struck by the typically Protestant questions that Ronald Eyre insisted on asking. He seemed fixated on 'piercing the facade' of Catholic practice. He appeared perplexed, even dismayed, by the affluence of St. Peter's and the ostentation of the applauding crowds gathered in the Square to receive the pope's blessing. He concluded that this really could not be true Catholic Christianity. Accordingly, he decided that the facade must be pierced so that we could see through the appearance to the reality. Eyre sought — to change the metaphor — the true kernel of Catholic faith hidden inside the husk of the dramatic, prepossessing external displays of processions, images, paintings, choirs and architecture.

First, he went to the Benedictine Abbey of Saint Anselmo in Rome. In the tranquility of the cloister, he tried to put the American abbot on the spot by asking how the opulence of the Roman Catholic Church might be reconciled with the Gospel's portrait of the material simplicity of Jesus' life. In addressing this question it is necessary to distinguish between Roman Catholic tradition, which is an historical, sociological reality, and a normative judgement about 'true' Christianity. It is very difficult for us — certainly in a survey like this — to decide what true Christianity is. For our purposes we should abandon the quest for true Christianity and concentrate on understanding the living, historical, and social reality at the heart of the Roman Catholic tradition. Adopting this perspective it becomes misleading to say, 'Let us pierce the facade'. The kind of Catholicism that we saw in St. Peter's Square and Cathedral and in the Shrine of the Black Madonna at Monserrat are integral parts of Roman Catholic tradition.

We may talk of different aspects of Catholic tradition. Viewed from one perspective the Catholic tradition discloses one set of features. Seen from another vantage point the Church discloses other, often quite strikingly different, qualities. This is not a matter of penetrating the facade to discover the true kernel buried therein. It is instead recognizing that, given its historical complexity, Roman Catholicism displays different facets or aspects. One is the Nazarene simplicity of the Little Brothers of Christ, the followers of Charles de Foucault. Another is the rich, ornate liturgy of St. Peter's and of Monserrat. What we saw in the Benedictine Abbey of Saint Anselmo, or what one sees in any local parish, is yet another aspect.

We may clarify the issue by noting that there is a similarity of structure between Roman Catholicism and Hinduism (and I daresay this would be true of most religions). Each tradition comprises diverse aspects that correlate with different subjective needs and psychological types. There are probably as many Catholics who are perplexed, not to say offended, by what they see in St. Peter's as there are Protestants from a British chapel tradition like Ronald Eyre's. Such Catholics strive to recover a gospel simplicity that would make them, in some respects, indistinguishable from some Quakers. The point is that when you are looking not at the revealed truth as such but at traditions as they have unfolded in history, it becomes very problematic to say that one form is true and another false. Historically speaking, they are all authentic forms of the religious tradition. One might want to raise the normative question as to which form is closest to the mind of Jesus Christ or to the gospel narratives. This, however, is a different question on which I am not going to take sides. It is a question of faith which varies among devotees. Questions about the truth of a presumptive revelation cannot be handled in a descriptive course such as this. Rather than dealing with questions of ultimate truth, our focus is on questions of historical and social manifestation.

A suggestion frequently made is that all this ecclesiastical pomp and glory is appropriated from the classical Roman culture. This may be true in a proximate, historical sense but, ultimately, it springs from the human heart. There is in human hearts — perhaps the majority — a hankering after a vision of truth in spectacular forms. How else are ornate and awesome architectural monuments that mark world civilizations to be explained? Whether it is the Bad Shahi Mosque in Lahore, the Taj Mahal at Agra, the Lakshmi Temple of Madurai, the giant stupa at Annaradhapura, the pyramids at Geza, the temple columns at Karnak, or the cathedrals at Salisbury and Rheims — all testify to a shared disposition in humankind's history. Accordingly, I doubt that we can say that the triumphalist sort of Catholicism that is so widespread derives only from the Roman matrix of its origins. The reason an historical catalyst can be so efficacious in catching hold of the piety and imagination of people is that it appeals to something deep in the human psyche.

God's Incarnation in Christ

We turn now to consider the central claim made for Roman Catholicism, the claim to which we were introduced in the cloistered garden of Saint Anselmo in Rome, namely, that Christ is divine. Christ's advent into the world is in reality the entry of God into history to change the historical process. As a result of the Christ event, divine grace is now available in human history — in the human world of space and time — in a new and decisive way. We are talking here, in other words, of incarnation. Incarnation means, first of all, the enfleshment of God. God takes humanity upon himself in the fullness of time by being born of a woman, the Virgin Mary. The result is that divine life is now available to human beings in a decisive, life-transforming, redemptive way. That affirmation, Father Wheatland explained in the Saint Anselmo cloister, is the crux which cannot be sacrificed without abandoning the core message of Christianity.

Other traditions, of course, make claims for incarnation. The Hindu tradition has no embarrassment whatsoever talking about godmen, several of whom I have visited in India. Christians are sometimes embarrassed in claiming that God became man; Hindus say it happens all the time. The entry of God into human form is not a rare event in Hindu perspective. In Christianity, on the contrary, the incarnation of God is held to be a once-for-all event. God has enfleshed himself once, and once only. It did not happen before and it will not happen again. At that point, we see the radical difference between the Hindu and Catholic doctrines of incarnation.

Concept of Grace

This discussion of incarnation serves to introduce the concept of grace. Mrs. Dryhurst had some difficulty explaining grace to Ronald Eyre during their chat in her kitchen. *Grace* basically means kindness and help from another. In fact, it is possible to schematize religious traditions in terms of their advocacy of what we might call *auto-salvation* over against *hetero-salvation*. Auto-salvation means you save yourself. An example might be the Buddha's last words, 'All composite things decay; therefore, strive earnestly.' In other words, know the truth and apply it for yourselves. The Buddha — at least in this Theravada tradition — is not a divine saviour. The bodhisattvas especially become cosmic saviours later in the Mahayana traditions. But in the normative Theravada tradition (though the piety of the masses may be something else) the Buddha is only a way-shower. None can save you; you must save yourself. This is auto-salvation.

But there is another way of being religious, and that is to rely on salvation by another. The vast majority of humankind has practised such hetero-salvation, or salvation by an outside agency. The *bhakti* or devotional tradition of Hinduism is a case in point. There may be a small number of Advaita Vedantins who maintain that spiritual emancipation comes by one's own discipline or yoga, attainment of wisdom and enlightenment. But the vast majority of

Hindus and Buddhists believe in salvation by another. The divine being graciously comes and does for them what they by their own resources are unable to do. They become transformed from the darkness of ignorance to the light of knowledge, from sin to salvation, from bondage to freedom, from death to immortality.

The doctrine of grace in Christianity is saying the same thing. Humans cannot save themselves but they need have no fear; God in his mercy and compassion has come to do in and for them what they cannot do in their own power. God, while we were yet sinners, has sent Jesus Christ to die for us so that we might be transformed from death to life. That is grace. It is the grace of God entering human history and the lives of individual human beings to take them from plight to transformation, from a condition gone wrong to a condition of rightness. In the Christian scheme the condition of rightness is reconciliation, that is, the restoration of relationship with God and with one's neighbour.

When Mrs. Dryhurst was talking about the paradox of the crucifixion as pain and glory, she suggested that a ready analogy of God's grace is to be found in a parent's love. It has always struck me, even in my most cynical moments, that if one were looking for some manifestation of human decency that could ground hope for the world, one would look at parental love. In a parent's love (though Mrs. Dryhurst spoke specifically of a mother's love) you see grace. There you discern a willingness to sacrifice, to dismiss pain, and to forget narcissistic aims of self-development and self-fulfillment in order to give life and blessing to the life of one for whom one is responsible. That, for her, was an analogy or a paradigm of grace. Grace is God's kindness, God's willingness to spend himself to the limit of the cross, in order to restore the beloved, that is to say, the fallen human creation.

Faith and Morality

A last facet of Catholic piety, seen preeminently in the Little Brothers of Christ, is the correlation between faith and morality. The Little Brothers of Christ clearly are convicted by the insight that faith without works is dead; that it is necessary for faith to issue in moral action on behalf of others. The faith of the Christian devotee must become incarnate in works of suffering and service that parallel those of the incarnate God, Jesus Christ. The Brothers devote themselves to homely ways of human service in the factory, in the barnyard, even in the garbage collection. Their example is very attractive and uplifting. It is reminiscent of the kind of life lived by Mother Theresa in the slums of Calcutta.

A caveat might be raised whether the sacrificial service of the Little Brothers of Christ restricts itself only to works of personal succour and of personal rehabilitation when they seek to be a Christian presence to individuals who are perplexed and dismayed, vexed in heart and body, on the factory assembly line or in the dye works. Does their moral concern extend also to a confrontation with what we might call social or systemic evil? One of the great values of the Canadian Catholic bishops' declaration entitled, 'Ethical Reflections on the Economic

Crisis', is that it clearly grasps the power of structural evil operative in human societies. The Catholic bishops are saying that it is not sufficient, although it may be necessary and worthwhile, to pick up the broken bodies after they have been smashed by poverty, unemployment, and preventable disease. One must try to change — to redeem in some finite historical way — those social, economic and political structures which are instrumental in diminishing humanity and destroying life. Accordingly, alongside the works of personal rehabilitation and sacrificial service of the Little Brothers of Christ, one must also put the vision of the Canadian Catholic bishops: 'This you ought to have done and not left the other undone.' The Christian disciple must also try to transform social, political and economic structures. Otherwise, as Bonhoeffer pointed out, they are simply picking up the broken bodies at the bottom of the dangerous mountain curve, instead of putting a barrier on the curve that prevents them leaving the road in the first place to crash below.

Here we must end our exploration of some dimensions of Roman Catholic tradition and faith.

A Perspective on
Eastern Orthodox Christians

THE ROMANIAN SOLUTION

Ronald Eyre issues a rebuke at the beginning of the film that we in the West overlook the 150 million Eastern Orthodox Christians in the world. This is generally a valid claim. It certainly is a correct characterization of my own experience. Though I knew Eastern Orthodoxy existed, I grew up knowing very little about it. A school friend's father was a priest of the Ukrainian Orthodox Church. Driving west along highway 401 towards Toronto past the automobile production plants of Oshawa, one espies the onion-shaped cupolas and distinctive cross of the Eastern Orthodox churches. Just east of the bicycle path along the Rideau River in Ottawa, glimpses may be caught of the distinctive architecture of the Eastern Orthodox Church.

Theological Issues in the Schism

The fact that we tend to know little about Eastern Orthodox Christianity is a legacy that goes back to the split of 1054 when the papal delegate, perhaps acting unofficially, laid a bull of excommunication

on the altar of the Byzantine Church, the Hagia
Sophia (Church of the Holy Wisdom) in Constantinople (now called Istanbul). The result was a
mutual excommunication. From that time, the
eastern Greek church and the western Latin church
have gone separate ways. That was the culmination
of a history of tension and conflict between
Constantinople and Rome.

There were theological differences, some of
which may now strike us as rather trivial. One
church historian wrote that Christendom was split
over a dipthong (a Greek grammatical stress). The
Creed of Nicaea was the result of a council called by
Constantine in 325 to define Christian doctrine in
the face of the Aryan heresy. But different interpretations emerged. In defining the identity of
Christ in relationship to the one God, the Western
church declared him to be *homoousion*, that is, of one
(or of the same) substance with the Father. The
Eastern church favoured the interpretation of
homoiousian, namely, that Christ was of a similar
substance with the Father. There are other differences. The Western church added to the Nicene Creed
the *filioque* phrase, 'and the Son.' In trying to define
the triune nature of God, the Western church said
that the Holy Spirit proceeds from God the Father
and the Son. The Eastern church resisted the inter-
polation of the *filioque* phrase. Firstly, it had not
been in the original formulation of the Creed of
Nicaea and, secondly, it seemed to them
presumptuous of the Latin church to act inde-
pendently of the whole church. Moreover, to
describe the procession of the Spirit from the Father

and the Son suggested two ultimate divine sources which would contradict monotheism. As in many theological debates, it is difficult to know whether this different form of words betrays a genuine and important difference in understanding or, on closer analysis, reflects only an apparent controversy.

Ecclesial and Social Factors

The schism, it should be noted, was not simply a doctrinal controversy between persons with different theological understandings of Christian truth. The Eastern church also resented what they thought was the illegitimate exercise of authority on the part of the Latin church and the pope specifically. One of the fundamental questions in religion is: what is the seat of authority? The question is not just what is the truth but how do you know that it is the truth? To what or to whom do you appeal in defense of a claim that something is true or good? The Eastern church resisted the Latin church's arrogation of authority to the pope. They were prepared to recognize the bishop of Rome as perhaps first amongst equals; they would not, however, concede supremacy to the pope as the authoritative definer of Christian doctrine. This function belonged exclusively to the councils of the church. Ronald Eyre alluded to seven ecumenical councils which the Eastern church regards as alone authoritative for a correct understanding of Christian teaching.

The problem with the Western or Latin church, in the eyes of Eastern Orthodoxy, is that it went on defining beyond the seven ecumenical councils. Ecumenical means world-wide or universal and indicates those councils in which the whole un-divided church participated. Ultimately, the church was divided over the question of authority, the Eastern church appealing to the ecumenical councils and the Latin church relying on the authority of the pope, the successor of Peter, as the guarantor of Christian truth. There are other social and political reasons for the continuing rupture, such as the crusades which left a legacy of conflict and hostility. The crusaders, on their way to and from the Holy Land, often ravaged Byzantine centres and, on one occasion, sacked the city of Constantinople.

A consequence of the rupture between the East-ern church centred in Constantinople (with its Greek language legacy and later becoming in great measure a Slavic-speaking church), and the Latin (or Western) church based in Rome, is the tragic ignorance that continues even to this day. There are, however, signs of it being overcome.

Orthodox Spirituality

Let us try now to get some insight into the distinc-tive quality of Eastern Orthodox spirituality. Our presentation is not interested principally in histori-cal questions, but in the problem of present mean-ing. Given the fact that there are approximately 150 million Orthodox Christians and that Romania pos-sesses a rich deposit of religious tradition and fer-vour, it behooves us to explore the character of the spiritual ethos or piety of Romanian Orthodox Christians to whom we were introduced.

Ikons

Our clue, as Ronald Eyre perceived at the beginning of the film, is the ikon. A magnificent white-bearded priest explained to Ronald Eyre that the ikons are adored, that the devotees' relationship to the ikon is not, as Ronald Eyre provisionally suggested, the relationship that one has towards a friend. 'No,' said the priest with great delicacy, 'it is a special adoration or relation.' The word 'adoration' may be misleading in that it suggests a worship of the ikon. If he had been a native English speaker, the priest undoubtedly would have used the word 'veneration', a word that stands for an appropriate reverential but limited relationship to something that is not God. 'Adoration' is usually used for the distinctive relationship of worship which is due God alone. One of the conflicts between the Eastern and Western church was the iconoclastic controversy regarding the appropriateness of ikons for Christian piety. The conclusion ultimately was that they should not be adored, for then they would be idols taking the place that is properly God's alone. They were instead to be venerated, serving to focus devotional feeling for the Orthodox.

There has already been enough exposure to bring home the point that this fervent, devotional use of images is not a unique phenomenon. Common structures may be discerned in religious phenomena. In Hindu tradition, the devotees routinely stroke and kiss religious images. The National Art Gallery in Ottawa contains a collection of Indian bronzes to which I occasionally take students. The curator explained to us that it was difficult to appreciate the original fine work of the images and even, in some cases, to identify them with precision because they had been worn away by the tactile piety of the devotees. The notion that a concrete material thing can be, as the Orthodox priest said 'a window to heaven' is a common form of consciousness amongst humankind. In Islamic tradition, veneration typically focuses on the black stone set in a corner of the *ka'ba* in a silver collar or frame which has to be replaced from time to time because of erosion caused by pilgrims stroking and kissing it. The same phenomenon may be observed in Rome where the large toe of the image of St. Peter is worn smooth by the devotional touches of the faithful. Finally, we see it in Romanian Eastern Orthodoxy in the underlying notion that the ikon can focus the transcendent presence that is not normally accessible because God dwells in mystery. God becomes temporarily available to the devotees through the ikon.

Believing and Worshipping

The foregoing discussion serves to introduce an important consideration, namely, that the principal activity of most religious people is not believing but worshipping. There is a tendency, when we meet people of a different tradition whose faith we seek to understand, to ask, 'What do you believe?' Alternatively, we objectify them in the third person and say, 'What do they believe?' The more proper question should be, as Remus (Ronald Eyre's guide) said, 'Whom do they worship?' That is the more profound and revealing question.

It is rare for believing to be the principal religious activity. By *believing* I mean assent of the mind to a set of propositions which are thought to be more or less correct representations of reality. In the Eastern Orthodox case there is the conviction that the universe does not exist autonomously, but that it is the result of divine intention. This may be expressed as an intellectual proposition or doctrine about the existence of a Creator God. Then there is a narrative of what this Creator God did. He came to earth in the flesh, born in a stable. He was baptized in the River Jordan. He preached and taught for three years and performed miracles. He died on a cross in a vicarious, atoning death. He was raised triumphantly. All this is displayed in the religious ikons. It could also be rendered in propositional form. Then it could be said that to believe means to say *yes* with the intellect to these propositions about that Creator God coming to earth and performing various redemptive acts. I am proposing that the activity which is called 'believing' (saying *yes* with the intellect to certain statements or doctrines that can be written down in a notebook and that can be read in a textbook) is not the chief activity of religious people. Some people believe very little because they have neither the capacity nor the disposition to worry their heads about doctrines. What they do instead is engage in a rich worship life. As Remus declared about the meaning of Christ's death and resurrection: 'Words do not suffice; they cannot convey the real meaning of what we feel.'

Similarly, the chief activity for Muslims is not theologizing, not believing with the head or assenting with the mind, but is, rather, the practice of God's law. The same thing is true of Jews. The principle activity is not believing or assenting with the mind to certain doctrines, but participating in a form of life which is viewed as divine law. In various historical traditions we see that believing is not the principal thing religious people do. In fact, the Christian creed (which is often rendered — 'We believe in one God, the almighty maker of heaven and earth' — should more properly be rendered, 'We worship one God, the almighty maker of heaven and earth.'

The Eastern Orthodox experience clarifies this point about the nature of belief; the chief thing they do is worship, making wide use of ikons to focus their devotion on God. Remus said to Ronald Eyre, 'Orthodoxy should not be translated as *right doctrine* [which will probably be the first dictionary definition you will find if you look it up] but, rather, *right praise.*' To be an Orthodox Christian is to praise or worship God in the right way.

Liturgy of the Bread and Wine

We look now at a particular dimension of Orthodox worship, specifically at the liturgy of the bread and wine. Liturgy is a Greek word which means the work or the service that people owe and give God. The work that they do is to participate in the rich ritual life of their tradition. The liturgy of the bread and wine, the eucharist, is also practised by Catholics and Protestants. What is distinctive about the Eastern Orthodox celebration of the ritual of the bread and wine is the context of mystery in which that ritual is placed.

The worshippers in the church are separated from the altar by a screen (*ikonostasis*), a kind of wall that goes across the church and which is covered with ikons. At a dramatic point in the ritual, the priest disappears inside, closes the doors, and pulls the drapes. The consecration of the bread and wine proceeds, hidden from the gaze of the faithful. Then the priest emerges through the doors of the *ikonostasis* bearing the gifts of God, the consecrated bread and wine, which have now become the body and blood of Christ the Saviour.

This hidden aspect of the ritual, that is, performing part of the ritual away from the direct sight of the devotees or congregation behind the screen, is an attempt to register upon the imagination what is only feebly said to the intellect with concepts. In other words, the sacred mystery is acted out. The priest could stand there until he is blue in the face pontificating about the mysterious transcendence and holy otherness of God. Instead, he acts it out in a way that appeals to the dramatic capacities of the imagination. Behind the screen the secret things of God are done. What this says to persons (in the language of symbolic communication) is that there is an ineffable depth to reality. There is a dimension of beyondness to the character of God that cannot be grasped with fragile and fragmentary words. We will never truly be able to get an intellectual handle on the mystery of God. As the priest passes through the doors of the *ikonostasis* we are told that, 'Definitions stop and you worship.'

To revert to comparativist allusions once again, it should be recalled how, in Hindu practice, the deity is frequently hidden in the *garba-graha*, the inner sanctum, the holy of holies. In many Hindu temples the God is not out there for ready, immediate profane observation. Instead, you have to stoop down under a lintel and go into the darkness where the image of the god is kept and lit up, if at all, by sputtering lamps. There you circumambulate the image of the god, remembering always that for the devotees the image is not just a mass of stone or bronze. The image is the god temporarily present in his or her image form. These actions in the darkness are symbolic, bringing home to the imagination of the devotee that there are mysterious dimensions or depths to the ultimate reality that he or she cannot comprehend. This sense of the mysterious reaches of God permeates the Eastern Orthodox enactment of the ritual of the bread and wine — surrounded as it is by light, colour, incense and the sacred, but penetrable, barrier of the *ikonostasis*.

The Non-Rational Element in Religion

In connection with this discussion of the sentiment of divine mystery and otherness, we should note the work of Rudolf Otto. In 1917, he wrote an important book called *The Idea of the Holy*. The purpose of this book was to bring home to his readers the consciousness of the non-rational dimension of God. Otto argued that Western Christianity is very rich in rational and moral concepts. Western theologians have devoted most of their energy to formulating what were intended to be increasingly precise specifications of the nature of God, humanity, and the relationship between them. These do not, how-ever, exhaust the totalilty of the godhead for there is a non-rational dimension which we tend to lose sight of. Otto argued that the word 'holy' might have represented this non-rational dimension of God if it were not that the word 'holy' has been pre-empted by ethical overtones. The word 'holy' immediately generates in people's minds associations of moral propriety. Accordingly, Otto coined the word 'numinous' (from the Latin *numen* — a divinity) to stand for God in that mysterious, non-rational dimension. The numinous signifies God in his awe-inspiring mysteriousness which, at the same time, fascinates and attracts us (*mysterium tremendum et fascinans*). The core of religion, Otto claimed, is not the rational concepts of theological doctrines or moral codes but, rather, the non-rational human feelings of awe, majesty, overpoweringness and fas-cination which correlate with the non-rational, transcendent depths of God.

The rational corresponds to certain concepts, beliefs or doctrines like 'God the Father, the al-mighty maker of heaven and earth who is all wise, who is everywhere and always present, a God who is all powerful.' The rational element of religion can be illustrated further by moral propositions like 'God is perfect righteousness'. The non-rational cannot be formulated in such concepts. Instead, the human correlate would be feelings, distinctive sentiments of awesomeness, of being overpowered, of majesty. Otto's analysis of the numinous remains one of the most influential reminders in modern western thought that there is an element of mystery that is primal in the religious life. This point which we have discussed here intellectually, the Eastern Orthodox act out in their rituals. There is a transcendent depth and mystery to God symbolized by the hiddenness of certain aspects of the Eucharistic liturgy.

Monasticism

Let us turn now to the phenomenon of Eastern orthodox monasticism. We have already a fair acquaintance with the phenomenon of the holy person (usually a man as it turns out) who has a special vocation. We met the Hindu sanyasin, the renunciant, who withdrew from everyday life (having been a lawyer) in the village of Bithbagwanpur. This provides some insight into the notion of someone who withdraws from normal, domestically engaged life, in order to devote himself to a special spiritual vocation. We observed the Theravada Buddhist monks of Sri Lanka who are the paradigms for the laity of what the spiritual life ultimately must be for all persons. The Roman Catholic monks, the Little Brothers of Jesus, provided us with further evidence of the religious phenomenon of monasticism.

Now we encounter the monks of Eastern Orthodoxy and have occasion to note once again the significance of monasticism in the general religious life. The lay people come to the monastery; recall the visit of the school children. These are not monks who hide away, as do some Hindu sadhus or holy men. These monks are something like the Buddhist monks who are available to the laity for visitation, for counselling, and for teaching. We were introduced to one monk who was inspired to this calling when, as a school child, he visited one of the monasteries. The monk has a vocation, as Ronald Eyre suggested, to be a 'living ikon'. He serves as a symbolic manifestation of the ultimate. God, hidden in mystery, condescends to become perceptable in different ways. We took note of the revelatory power of the ikons and the symbolic ritual of the bread and wine. The presence of the monk also serves as a kind of conduit by which the divine impinges upon human life.

Sacralizing the Everyday

Another interesting facet of the film was the inter-penetration of the sacred dimension with everyday, so-called secular life. Our attention was directed to the spring housecleaning. This could be simply a pragmatic job of getting rid of the winter ashes and dust. If any of you are woodburners as I am, you know what an unholy mess it makes. You learn to close an eye to some of the accumulation of dust. But when spring comes you open all the doors and windows to get all of the gathered soot and ash out of your home. What could be purely a practical under-taking is invested with a special sacred meaning. That seems to be one of the magical tricks that is worked by religion. It sanctifies the everyday, as Martin Buber said. Religion takes everyday activities and makes them more than they are on the surface. Thus, spring housecleaning becomes a kind of spiritual preparation for Easter. The cleansing of the house symbolically represents (perhaps even symbolically brings about) the cleansing of the self as the faithful prepare to receive the presence of God in the Easter liturgy.

Christ and Culture

The Eastern Orthodox Christianity of Romania evinces a kind of fusion of culture with religion — a fusion of the sacred transcendent with the immanent secular. Beauty that appeals to the senses is used as a gateway to the divine. You should recall Ronald Eyre's rather sardonic query whether Romanians, if they had had an Oliver Cromwell, would have painted the walls of their richly decorated churches? The whole walls are really one enormous fresco depicting sacred heroes and biblical scenes.

Beauty that appeals to the senses is used to contemporize the presence of God. This may be observed also in the preparation of the Easter eggs. Perhaps there are even deeper mythical meanings there, for the egg is often a cross-cultural symbol of new life. Out of the egg comes the new life of the chicken. Accordingly, the egg represents the resurrection victory of Christ over sin, death, and ignorance, that makes possible a new spiritual life. There is the everyday (the egg) using culture (artistic decoration) to become a message of a divine promise (new life).

Another theme that emerges here (consistent with what I have been saying about the fusion of ordinary culture with sacred realities) is the connection between the philosophers of antiquity and the Christian revelation. Explaining the detail of that richly decorated church in Moldavia, Remus remarked: 'Here is Plato, Aristotle, Socrates.' You might well ask what they are doing on a church building. In the Orthodox outlook, however, the past does not have to be denigrated. The discoveries and the cultural achievements of the pre-Christian pagans are not repudiated in the light of the new revelation in Christ. Rather, what people thought before that was wise and true, what they have done that was good and beautiful can be appropriated by the Christians and assimilated into a new and comprehensive Christian synthesis. That is what the Eastern Orthodox have done.

That was not the only possibility in Christian history. One Latin thinker, Tertullian, in the second century rhetorically asked, 'What has Athens to do with Jerusalem?' (Athens symbolizes the Greek philosophers: Socrates, Plato and Aristotle. Jerusalem symbolizes the revelation of God in the history of Israel and Jesus Christ and his church.) The answer he gives, in effect, is, 'Nothing. Athens is but a garbage heap of Jerusalem. There is really nothing of value in the pre-Christian pagan philosophers and poets, so reject them and cling only to Christ.'

That certainly has not been the move made by the Roman Catholic Church nor by the Eastern Orthodox Church. Rather, they see these pre-Christian pagan philosophers and poets as forming a preparation for Christ. The technical word is *preparatio evangelica*, a preparation for the gospel. Whatever they said that is true and good should be seen as a way of preparing humankind for the final disclosure of God in Jesus Christ. Romanian

Orthodoxy displays hospitality towards pre-Christian classical culture, epitomized by the philosophers of antiquity.

The Easter Liturgy

Finally, the film deals with the Paschal liturgy, the liturgy of Easter. Bear in mind the long wait in the darkness and the first flicker of candlelight which the priest brings from within the church, then the light going from person to person as candles are lit from other candles, representing the interdependence of the community of believers. A strong sense of solidarity is demonstrated in the Eastern liturgy as the candles are lit one from the other. In so doing, they set forth the Easter mystery. This was anticipated in the ritual that took place on the Saturday before Easter — going low under the table which represented the tomb of Christ. When the participants pass under the table, they are with their own bodies reenacting a dominant Christian motif of dying with Christ, and then, on Easter, rising with Christ. They act out symbolically what is happening internally, spiritually. They die with Christ in the sense that they die to the old self of egocentricity, selfishness, fear, hostility, faithlessness, and mortality. They are raised to a new life of freedom, love, fellowship, and immortality.

All these meanings are enacted in the ritual. It seems that rituals are a universal way of not only showing pictures of truth messages but also of actually making things happen. That is something that outsiders sometimes have difficulty recognizing. Outsiders are, at their most generous, prepared to concede that the ritual may present a picture of the devotees' understanding of salvation. But, the devotees usually insist that it is not just a matter of giving a symbolic picture of truth. It is a matter of participating in truth, of transformative, salvific events actually happening. So, when they stoop low under the table, they are — inwardly and spiritually — dying with Christ and emerging Easter morning as transformed persons in possession of resurrection life.

A contemporary historian of religion who has brought this to our attention with great force is a Romanian, Mircea Eliade. He makes the point that in rituals there is a reenactment of a sacred past. Eliade dealt at great length with cosmogonic myths, myths that tell the stories of origins.

The conviction is held in many primitive societies, that the things that were done by the god(s) at the beginning serve to impart a particular structure or order or meaning to reality. The world is kept in a state of order, harmony, and balance by the rituals that reenact that past original creative event when God made the world. Thereby they continue to inspire the world with cosmic order or pattern in place of the chaos it would otherwise be. Similarly with the Romanian Paschal ritual. They are not here reenacting creation stories but, rather, the salvation story of the death and resurrection of Christ. In so doing, what happened once upon a time becomes a present reality for the devotee. There would, otherwise, be a great problem. If we allege an historical revelation (for example, that once upon a time when Augustus was emperor of Rome God came to earth), one might well ask what that has to do with us here and now in Ottawa or Thunder Bay, Moose Jaw or Port Hardy. The point of contact is, at least in one respect, the rituals we observed; the rituals contemporize that redemptive past. Take, for example, the atoning death of Christ; the people share his death by going into the tomb with Christ. The ritual further enacts the resurrection of Christ as the people at Easter dawn are suffused with new light as the candle flames go from one to the other; they are raised with Christ. The purpose of the liturgy is to make present here and now in the life of the devotee the salvation reality that historically occurred once upon a time in the life, death and resurrection of Jesus Christ.

What I have said about the Eastern Orthodox will generally be true of most religious traditions. They exist to contemporize ritually, past revelatory and saving events.

Christ and Communism

The film concluded with a discussion of the relationship between Communism and Christianity. I will not belabour that exchange. The suggestion was left that Christianity and Communism are not necessarily the irreconcilable enemies that are alleged by the kind of people at the Baptist Temple in Indianapolis, for whom Communism is the anti-Christ, for whom the Christian mission is to engage in a holy warfare against Communism.

Several years ago my wife and I went surreptitiously to a meeting of mainly right-wing movements in San Francisco. We encountered extreme manifestations of that Christian crusading spirit against Communism that is grounded in the assumption that Communism is atheistic and incommensurable with a tradition that teaches that the ultimate reality is a personal, loving father-mother God. Yet, there are suggestions at the end of the film that there is a certain compatibility between the social vision of justice, harmony and equality advocated by Marxists and the Christian dedication to a God whose prophets demand that justice should roll down like waters and righteousness like an ever-living stream. That is something that readers may want to explore at length on their own. I myself think that contemporary, liberation theologians (mainly on the Catholic side) who perceive a qualified compatibility between certain dimensions of Marxism and Christianity have got it right. There are those disturbing allusions in the Bible to a God who puts down the mighty from their thrones, who fills the poor with good things, and sends the rich away empty. The suggestions at the end from those Romanians, who were simultaneously Communist party members and devout Eastern Orthodox Christians, may in fact be a correct assessment of what is possible politically. In any case, it was a Romanian solution at the time the films was made. It is too early to tell what will be the effects on religious life of the unexpected and dramatic political changes in eastern Europe brought about by the democracy movement of the winter of 1989-90.

A Perspective
on Protestant Christians
PROTESTANT SPIRIT, U.S.A.

W e turn now to examine the meaning of Protestant Christian developments in the United States. My procedure will be to follow more or less the sequence of the film. This will result occasionally in some repetition but this simply reflects the oscillations of the film.

The Protestant Principle

Ronald Eyre begins with his own very general definition of what he calls the Protestant spirit. He declares that the Protestant spirit is characterized by an attitude in which all labels, institutions and structures are suspect. This is probably a percipient characterization of the Protestant ethos, and we shall return to it at the end. This general idea is encapsulated in a formula promulgated by an important contemporary Protestant theologian, Paul Tillich. When he sought to characterize the spirit of Protestantism, Tillich devised the formula, 'the Protestant Principle'. The Protestant principle is an attitude of criticism and judgement against all human, historical attainments. Nothing that human beings can achieve in their earthly pilgrimage can be absolutized, that is, can be deemed a final and perfect achievement. All human accomplishments — intellectual, moral, institutional, even religious ones — fall under a constant critique, imposed by the absolutely perfect will of the transcendent God.

This orientation of suspicion or criticism is, in my judgement, an incisive delineation of the spirit of Protestantism. More about this later.

When Martin Marty, a prominent American church historian at the University of Chicago, undertook to be Eyre's guide in the long search for the spirit of Protestantism, he led him first of all to a church in West Barnstable, in New England, and explained the reason for beginning the search at that point. The normative origins of Protestantism, Marty finds, are in a people gathered around the Bible to hear the word of God and to enjoy fellowship with one another. This experience lies at the core of Protestantism, certainly in its historical origins. Marty goes on to say that this originating ethos — a people gathered around the bible attentive to the word of God — has undergone a great deal of historical transmutation throughout the passage of time. Consequently, what we see nowadays is a highly diversified Protestantism. This contemporary diversity is exemplified by the city of Indiannapolis. The paradigm case for our understanding of American Protestantism is to be Indianapolis with its one million inhabitants, 50% of them black, and its 1100 churches.

Christ and Culture

We are immediately confronted with a panorama of the diversity, even grotesqueness, of Protestant Christianity in Indiannapolis. We hear a preacher exhorting everyone to believe that Jesus is the answer to all the world's ills. We have the paraphernalia of a certain kind of Protestantism: car bumper stickers exhorting people to honk if they love Jesus; combs with an inscription reminding the user that Jesus is the Lord; candles in the form of praying hands; and a plastic head of Christ which serves as a nightlight. In this hardware and bric-a-brac, characteristic of a certain kind of evangelical piety, we are introduced to a gaudy, Protestant equivalent to Lourdes. We encountered next a quite staid Protestant pastor, intoning in fairly typical Presbyterian or Methodist fashion as he read the scriptures.

In all this diversity we can, nevertheless, claims Marty, discern two main divisions. Protestantism sub-divides into two main classes which can be differentiated on the basis of the respective positions adopted on the question: what is the relation of Christ to culture? I am using the word 'Christ' here in a symbolic way to stand for the central Christian revelation, the essential or core Christian message, that is the authority for all faith and practice. We are asking, accordingly, what is the relationship of that authoritative revelational, transcendent core to general culture. It is scarcely possible to discuss this question without noting the landmark study of H. Richard Niebuhr called precisely, *Christ and Culture*. It is a book which reflects the scholarship of one who has mastered enormous historical materials and at the same time has the philosophical competence to categorize the sweeping range of historical data. Whereas Niebuhr differentiates five different categories of Christian relationship to culture, Marty isolates just two.

First of all, there are those Christians who are at home in the culture. These comprise the mainline churches. 'Mainline' here includes Presbyterians, Methodists, and Congregationalists which have, in large measure, been assimilated in Canada into the United Church of Canada. Also included are Episcopalians or Anglicans, and some Baptists and Lutherans, as well as others. The mainline churches are those with the big buildings that have stood for some time on the principal corners of North American city streets.

The usual term used to designate the type of thought shared by these mainline churches at home with their culture is liberalism. It is perhaps an ambiguous term, but it has been widely used in the past. I shall give below a very brief survey of some of the main characteristics of liberalism.

Over against this first group at home in the culture is the second group which Marty informs us are intent to rescue souls out of the culture, and to preserve them for heaven. This second main division feels that there is something inherently and irreparably wrong with the environing culture and the best one can hope for is a rescue operation which takes souls out of a corrupt and fallen, Satanic world, and inserts them into a new dimension of living which prepares them for the eternity of heavenly bliss. The second group is commonly called, and was so-called in the film, fundamentalism.

This might be the appropriate time to point out a high degree of ambiguity in Marty's characterization. He asserts that the second or fundamentalist group wishes to rescue people from historical existence, to take them out of the prevailing culture, and insert them into a special supernatural life which prepares them for heaven. I am somewhat perplexed by this because it has struck me for a long time that there is a peculiar identification of many fundamentalist churches with the dominant American culture. About thirty years ago I used to enjoy visiting fundamentalist churches and was intrigued by what struck me as a contradiction. On the one hand, they insisted that the 'saved' — those who had placed their faith in Jesus Christ — had come out of the world and were now separated from the contamination of a secular cultural sphere controlled by Satan. Yet, on the other, those same fundamentalists who insisted on their separation from the world, exhibited a style of life and worship which struck me as being embarassingly similar to many prevailing currents in the mainstream culture.

In evidence, we may note the young ladies of the film who sang in the Baptist temple, whose Pastor, Greg Dixon, had raised its membership from 300 to 7,000 members. They attacked Darwinian evolutionary theory by singing that their ancestors did not swing from a tree: 'I'm no kin to the monkey, and the monkey is no kin to me.' They then caricatured the ecumenical movement as containing communists and the devil. That act could be booked into

Barrymore's and it would go, because it has all of the jazzy style of modern nightclub culture. I observed the same phenomenon three decades ago. It has always struck me that the profession of separation of the saved from the contaminating culture is not borne out, at least not to the extent one might expect in light of the stridency of that profession, by the actual performance.

There is additional evidence in recent times that demonstrates the close affinity, at certain points, of fundamentalist Christianity with the prevailing culture. I am alluding to the emergence of the 'moral majority'. The moral majority had not emerged at the time that this film was made, but one could already see anticipations of it. This is a kind of thinking that holds that the American way of life is, at least in its founding inspiration, if not equivalent, then very close to the true meaning of the Christian gospel. We uncover a curious irony where the mainline American churches, which nowadays includes Roman Catholicism as well as Protestantism, become the institutions which are most censorious of prevailing political directions. It is the mainline churches who, in our own time, have most strongly condemned government policies concerning nuclear weapons and star wars, or the imperial Latin American policy of United States administrations.

This is a curious reversal of what we might have been led to expect. Many of the fundamentalist churches, which are, in principle, in enmity with the prevailing culture because it is unGodly, and are summoned by their allegiance to Jesus Christ to be separated from the world, turn out to be closely identified with the prevailing political trends of American foreign policy. The mainline churches, who are supposed to be at home in the culture, often find themselves at the cutting edge of opposition to the prevailing cultural axioms about the American way of life and the American responsibility to stand against alien ideologies.

Though there is a certain ambiguity to these definitions, I would agree that a useful principle for differentiating churches is that which distinguishes them on the basis of their understanding of the relation of the revelation in Christ to the general culture. When, however, one seeks to apply this basic criterion to specific churches and proceeds to identify those churches that are at home in the culture with the mainline denominations, and those which are hostile to the culture with fundamentalism, a great deal of murkiness is met which challenges such a simple equation.

Liberal Theology

Let me briefly turn now to delineate the main features of liberal, Protestant thought that characterizes the mainline churches, the kind of churches that are represented by North Methodist church in *The Long Search* film.

First is the principle of the immanence of God. Liberal theology's inspiration is largely in such prominent and influential nineteenth century theologians like Schleiermacher, Hegel, Baur, Strauss, Feuerbach, and Ritschl. The idea gained currency that God is not only, or not even principally, an utterly transcendent being, dwelling beyond this earth and intruding upon it only in highly selective revelatory and saving events, but, rather, that God is within the natural and historical processes of space and time.

Perhaps the most prominent influence was Hegel's notion of the Absolute Idea, or the universal Spirit, coming to full expression within the historical process. This Hegelian idea of divine immanence in history exerted a profound influence on Protestant thought. God was at work not only in the deeds that are recorded in the Bible — not only in the call of Abraham, or in Moses' leading of the people of Israel from bondage in Egypt in the exodus, or the giving of the law to Moses at Sinai — but also in what some would consider ordinary, everyday, profane history.

The notion that God is at work in an immanent way in nature has a logical link-up with evolutionary theory. It was argued by some liberal theologians that the belief in evolution does not necessitate the abandonment of belief in God, but simply a theological re-adjustment. The findings of biological science are to be interpreted as confirmation of God's manner of working within the evolutionary process to bring the human being from early, primal forms of life, to more mature forms of life, culminating ultimately in moral and spiritual fulfillment.

A second feature of liberal theology is its tendency towards a low Christology or a humanistic interpretation of the person of Christ. When the pastor of the fundamentalist church was asked what was central to the fundamentalist ethos, he replied that they had twenty-two beliefs which centred in the person of Jesus Christ. These begin with the affirmation that Jesus Christ is very God of very God, that is, that there is a true incarnation of God in Jesus Christ. This is a high Christology: Jesus is incarnate God. A low Christology is an interpretation of Jesus asserting that Jesus is a human being — though not just an ordinary one. Rather, he is the most perfect of human beings. Jesus serves as our moral exemplar, or, as Schleiermacher advocated, as our spiritual model because his is the most God-filled consciousness; in Jesus there is fullness of the sense of the presence of God. Jesus ought to serve as leader, as spiritual mentor, as moral exemplar, but he is not typically regarded by liberal theologians as the incarnation of the absolute God.

Another aspect of liberal theology, which has deeply influenced the mainline denominations, is the location of the authority for what one believes and what values one ought to prize in human experience. That experience can be the experience of reason or it can be the experience of emotion. The claim may be made that by thinking clearly, logically, upon the public data available to all persons without any special appeals to extraordinary means of divine self-disclosure, persons can arrive at truth. Or, alternatively, the conviction may be held by some liberals that the authority for belief and conduct may be found in certain feeling states. For Schleiermacher the important feeling that legitimates belief in God is the feeling of absolute dependence. The feeling of being dependent upon an infinite power is what underlies convictions about the existence of God.

Rudolf Otto also argued that authority is to be found in certain distinctive feeling states, which he characterized as *numinous*. This is a sense of being in the presence of awesome power, of being confronted with mystery which overpowers one but, at the same time, utterly fascinates. Otto called the source of this distinctive experience *mysterium tremendum et fascinans*, meaning the consciousness of mysterious reality that generates a feeling of holiness, that is, of awe and majesty, and yet does not repel but attracts the creature.

These are examples of that liberal outlook which finds authority in human experience — either rational or affective. In contradistinction, the fundamentalists would claim to find the seat of authority in the Bible alone. This is a critical difference in perspective.

Liberals tend, further, to be optimistic about human nature. Fundamentalists tend to stress the utter sinfullness of human beings. This perspective has certain interesting connections with the preceding point about biblical authority. The liberals typically view the Bible as a human record of God's historical interaction with Israel and the Church, a record which includes a prominent element of culturally conditioned human thinking. Accordingly, when liberals interpret the story of the Fall of Adam in the book of Genesis, they do not treat it as an historical account. Fundamentalists, on the contrary, regard the Genesis stories as absolutely literal, historical statement of how things originated including human sin. For them, the sin that Adam and Eve committed in defying God and eating the forbidden fruit is biologically transmitted to all their descendents. Thus is the whole human race, inevitably and profoundly, corrupted by sin.

The point I wish to make here is that there is a connection between the way scripture is exegeted or interpreted, and the doctrinal implications one discovers. On the question of what is the nature of a human being, liberals tend to be optimistic. They hold that with will power, rational effort and discipline, a good life can be created on earth. As a corollary of that, there is a belief in social progress. This confidence in historical progress clearly correlates with an optimistic judgment about human possibilities. Good people, admittedly with the help of God's revelation and spirit, can achieve a peaceful and just state of affairs here on earth. It may not quite be heaven, but it will be sufficiently pleasant that Christians need not hanker after heaven prematurely. Humans can create a decent society on earth: a comfortable state of affairs where there is food, shelter, medicine and security for all.

This ideal of social progress has led to the social gospel, which Ronald Eyre characterized as a fundamentalist's nightmare when he found himself in a social action committee of North Methodist Church, whose members were listening to a young offender talk about the program he was initiating to steer young people away from crime. That kind of social activism or social gospel is the kind of alleged deviation from Christian faith in personal salvation that causes fundamentalists to condemn the mainline, or liberal churches.

Fundamentalist Reaction

The forgoing is a cursory sketch of the kind of liberal Christianity against which fundamentalism reacted. Fundamentalism is a term which emerged at the beginning of the century when certain Christian people sought to recall Christendom from what they regarded as the heresy of liberal thought to the 'fundamentals' of the Christian revelation. We may see that fundamentalism exhibited in the Baptist temple in Indiannapolis.

When the pastor of the congregation was pressed as to their key doctrine, he replied that it was the doctrine about the Bible. It was not, as one might have thought, the doctrine about Christ — his incarnation and vicarious death or the substitution-ary atonement, his bodily resurrection and bodily ascension to heaven, or his bodily return again on the clouds of heaven — but, rather, the doctrine of biblical revelation. The Bible, as the pastor of the Baptist temple explained, is verbally inspired by God; God speaks the words that are in the Bible. It is not a human invention; not even a product of the most elevated human consciousness. The Bible comes from the mind of God. Therefore it is to be believed literally.

Few, if any, of the the mainline churches would make that statement. They have appropriated the nineteenth century historical criticism of the Bible which claims that the Bible does not come full-blown from the mind of God. The Bible is an historical document which reflects its context and culture. In other words, the Bible has an earthly history; it is not a sudden irruption from a supernal realm.

The fundamentalist notion of the Bible resembles in many respects the Muslim conception of the revelation of God in the Qur'an. For Muslims, God's final revelation is the holy book which communicates one of his attributes called the speech of God. The Qur'an is word for word, the speech of God, duplicating an eternal Qur'an in Heaven. The Qur'an on earth, written in Arabic, mirrors this mother of the book as it is called, written on preserved tablets in heaven. This Islamic conception of scriptural revelation is analogous to Protestant fundamentalist views of the bible.

Liberals, while not disputing that the Bible contains divine revelation, would not assert that it is a verbally inspired book. The Bible is not itself — word for word — the Christian revelation. Rather, they would incline towards the view that the revelation consists of God's mighty deeds among the people of Israel and the early church, predominantly in Christ and his apostles. The Bible contains the record of revelation, that is to say, the record of those historical events in which God originally disclosed himself. As such, it is also the human prism through which the ever-living God continues to reveal himself to successive generations.

In trying to understand fundamentalism, we may isolate the theory of evolution because it featured so prominently in the film. The Darwinian notion of evolution asserts that nature exhibits a struggle for survival. Those species which survive are those selected by nature as best adapted to particular circumstances.

The fundamentalists attack this Darwinian evolutionary theory for several reasons. They reject it, first of all, because it seems to many devout Christians that it contradicts Christian understanding of a human being. They feel that the pre-eminence of the human creature in God's creation can only be maintained if Adam (and humanity) is the result of a special act of creation as the Bible depicts. In one biblical version God fashions a human image out of the dust of the earth, inspirits that dust with his divine breath; the result is a living person. Some fundamentalists feel that if humans are not the result of such a special divine creative act, their status is diminished. If humans are really simply a complex animal in continuity with the 'monkeys', then the conviction of the distinctiveness of the human created in the image of God is lost.

Another reason fundamentalists have attacked the idea of evolution is because it seems to challenge their faith in the providential care of God. The struggle for survival is a cruel mechanism for achieving a purpose. Fundamentalists believe that human destiny is the result of God's loving care and not the consequence of a chancy process of natural selection in the struggle for survival.

The point of resistance that was stressed in the film was the status of the scriptures. It was argued by the fundamentalist pastor that to hold to evolution is to deny the authority of the bible which relates the true way the world and humans were brought into being by God. To question this account in Genesis is totally unacceptable to a fundamentalist perspective, which sees the disclosure of God in an absolutely authoritative way in the Bible.

One of the attractive features of fundamentalism is that it has grasped, at least on the level of profession, that religion necessarily includes an appeal to personal transformation. Religion is meaningless if it does not entail this summons to move out of an unreal, profane state of existence into the real, sacred world and a true way of life. Fundamentalism, with its constant exhortation to become saved, retains what is essential to any proper understanding of what religion is and how it functions, namely, an appeal to transformation. This is not to say that mainline churches do not include it but they generally include it in a less obvious way. The fundamentalist is highly articulate about it. The good life, a fulfilled life, requires a dramatic movement from the broken, sorrowful, profane existence, in which humans inescapably find themselves, to a new and true way of life. That is an important stress which is essential to any authentic understanding of religion. The fundamentalists seem to understand this — at least on the rhetorical level.

The Gospel of Total Liberation

I shall leap now to the Mount Vernon Baptist Church, because it is clear that both Ronald Eyre and Martin Marty are most entranced by what they find there. I can empathize deeply with that, because at a certain stage of my life, I received much joy from going to black churches. I have worshipped in black churches in New Orleans, Detroit, Newburg, New York and Windsor, Ontario. Besides enjoying the compelling music, I was moved by the sense of ecstasy that seemed to permeate the assemblies. This hearkens back to what was said above about transformation. Ecstasy comes from the Greek *ek-stasis* and signifies being lifted out of where one normally stands into another dimension. In a religious context, ecstasy means the exaltation that accompanies conversion from a condition of sin, guilt, suffering, ignorance and death to a state of truth, goodness, wholeness and immortality.

There is a ready explanation for this sense of authenticity in the black experience: the Gospel itself is aimed principally at the poor and the dispossessed. I often wonder how people who allege to be Christians can read the Bible and still carry on in their normal ways of getting and spending. The Bible talks about God putting down the mighty from their thrones and exalting those of low degree. He fills the hungry with good things, and the rich he sends empty away (Luke 1:52-3). This is a radical Gospel of personal and social transformation which is biased in favour of the poor and the oppressed. When Jesus came to the synagogue in Nazareth where he had been brought up, he read from the scroll of the prophet Isaiah:

> The Spirit of the Lord is upon me, because he has anointed me to preach good news to the poor. He has sent me to proclaim release to the captives and recovering of sight to the blind, to set at liberty those who are oppressed, to proclaim the acceptable year of the Lord (Luke 4 : 18-19).

This liberating, succouring perspective is so built into the Christian message that one can understand why people, who experientially know in their bones what dispossession, poverty, injustice and oppression is, would resonate to the Gospel. The Gospel was tailor-made for them. Perhaps that is why we get that sense of authenticity in churches like Mount Vernon Baptist Church.

This church also has a social conscience; its members provide Thanksgiving turkey dinners for some 2,000 people. Perhaps more importantly is Pastor Mose Saunders' organization of OIC — Opportunities Industrialization Centres. He considers this social outreach to be a mission; the church without OIC would not be the church; OIC without the church would not be OIC. There is a strong sense of social entailment in their understanding of the Christian message. The Christian task is not simply a rescue operation of souls, plucking them from this corrupt and degenerate world of space and time in the grip of Satan, and holding them in abeyance until the second coming of Christ when they will be resurrected and share his glory in Heaven. It includes this element of personal salvation but it has the additional dimension of social transformation. There are no evident signs in the film that the thrust for social transformation extends also to the political realm. However, the growing black involvement in the American political process may, in some cases, be understood as the extension of the social implications of the Gospel into the political realm as well.

At the conclusion Martin Marty claims to understand why Ronald Eyre should be drawn back, time and time again, to Mount Vernon Baptist Church. The spirit of Protestantism, which has been moving from place to place over the centuries since 1517 when Luther nailed his theses to the church door at Wittenburg, now finds its abode in the kind of church movement exhibited by Mount Vernon Baptist Church.

Conclusion

In summing up his understanding of Protestantism, Ronald Eyre says that what Protestantism finally stands for is not a specified number of doctrines, twenty-two or however many, which must be believed. Nor is the Protestant ethos defined by a reified institution, that is, an institution with a divinely established and fixed order of ministry whether defined as rule by elders or bishops. Neither is Protestantism a set form of worship mandatory for all devotees. Rather, it is a critical spirit that becomes agitated whenever it discerns hardening of ecclesiastical arteries. Wherever it sees rigidity setting in, wherever it detects a set of doctrines becoming fixed and final, or a form of church government becoming authoritative for all, or a style of worship being imposed on all, in other words, wherever it sees idolatry — a human achievement, ecclesiastical, doctrinal, moral, liturgical being assigned, often unconsciously, absolute status — then the spirit of Protestantism cries out *Halt.* It refuses to identify the absolute and perfect will of a transcendent God with any relative human achievements — even worthy ones. It is an impulse to keep things moving in an ongoing process of becoming. Many Protestants like to define their church as *ecclesia reformata, et semper reformandum*, that is, a church which is reformed but still always in process of reforming itself.

A Perspective on Muslim Faith
THERE IS NO GOD BUT GOD

The presentation on the meaning of Islam begins with Ronald Eyre's visit to a mosque where we are introduced, first of all, to the grandeur of Muslim architecture, the great 1100 year old mosque of Ibn Talun and, second, the Muslim practice of ritual prayer.

Religious Diversity

A theoretical point that is useful in our understanding of all traditions, is brought home to us right at the outset. This is the reminder that there is a great deal of diversity within all traditions. There is a danger that we regard all traditions as monolithic systems of doctrine having a single meaning for all adherents, which scholars can grasp and delineate in tidy charts and catalogues. In fact, there is within every tradition a great deal of stubborn variety.

In this film, Ronald Eyre does not presume to speak for the whole of Islam, stretching from the Atlantic to Indonesia; rather, he declares his intention to understand Egyptian Islam. Earlier, I stressed that we must always proceed with caution when making statements about religious persons who participate in a tradition in which we do not. An even greater caution comes into play when we recognize that even within the religious community whose meaning we seek, there is likely to be a multiplicity of understandings. Admittedly, we may be able to extract a core meaning; we may be able to penetrate to an understanding of reality that characterizes all adherents of that particular tradition. Nevertheless, the particular forms in which that tradition and its meanings are going to be manifest will vary. What we are exposed to now is Egyptian Islam. Even more specifically, it is Egyptian Islam as refracted through an urban centre of power, and then Egyptian Islam as viewed through the prism of village life a hundred miles from Cairo.

To sum up my first general point which pertains to the study of all religions: be cautious about assuming that you have grasped the meaning of an entire tradition simply because you have been able to grasp a miniscule portion of the tradition in a particular person or historical period.

Religious Fusions

The second theoretical point that grows out of the preceeding one is to recognize that great world religions encourage this diversity by linking with local traditions. The tradition arising from the prophet Muhammad has resulted in the Islamicization of local cultures. The same thing happened with Christianity. We have had enough exposure to Christianity in both its Catholic and Protestant manifestations to recognize how diverse are these traditions. We have seen, for example, that the Catholicism of Spain at one of the great pilgrimage centres such as Monserrat differs from the simple life of the Little Brothers of Christ. We have seen how Protestant Christianity varies from large fundamentalist temples to the piety of black congregations. The genius, it seems, of all of the great world religions is to maintain elements of local traditions even as they are absorbed into the greater revelation. This process is sometimes called *syncretism*.

Buddhism has also done this. Buddhism moves from its birthplace in north central India, across the Gangetic plain to what is now Pakistan, to Gandhara. There it leaps across the great mountain passes of the Hindu Kush and the Karakoram and moves into Central Asia. There it undergoes transformation as it moves along the silk route into China and moves across the sea to Japan. Buddhism shares this capacity to baptize local cultures into the normative vision just as does Islam. Indonesian Islam is different from Egyptian Islam. What we are exploring is actually one small segment of the highly diverse, highly ramified Islamic tradition; the segment which is in Cairo and its adjacent village.

Existential Hermeneutic

A further methodological point should be made. (When I say theoretical, or methodological, point I mean a point that has pertinence to understanding religion in its entirety and not just one particular historical tradition.) Ronald Eyre was told that if he wanted really to know Islam he should become a Muslim. Now that could be said about all traditions.

If you want to understand Christianity, become a Christian. If you want to understand Buddhism, become a Buddhist. If you want to understand Hinduism, become a Hindu. It is what might be called an existentialist hermeneutic, meaning that if one wants to understand the inner meaning of symbols, that is, if one wants to understand how religious symbols transform life, how they inculcate reality-perceptions and values, then one has to get inside the tradition. Remaining on the outside, looking in, guarantees from the outset that the capacity to understand will be highly limited. What is said to Ronald Eyre about Islam could be correctly said about all religious traditions. If we want to understand them truly and deeply, if we seek to understand the symbols the way a devotee understands them, then we must, almost by definition, become participants in those traditions.

Even if one does not intend to get inside, it is the course of wisdom at least to understand how little one does know. If we do not intend to become participants, or if through lack of faith we are unable to become participants, then we should, first, realize the modesty of our claims for understanding and, secondly, we should employ a checking procedure by asking those who are insiders if they can recognize themselves in the kind of statements that we make about their faith. This salutary procedure is generally followed by Ronald Eyre throughout. Even when he takes quite naive stabs at grasping the meaning of a foreign tradition, he at least has the profound good sense to check it out. He tries to confirm his subjective insights into the meaning of a tradition by asking the authentic participants: Is this what it means when you do such and such, when you pray, when you give alms, when you go on pilgrimage? Is this what you see, what you feel? To the extent that he gets a confirmatory answer, he can then claim to have a preliminary understanding of that tradition even though he remains an outsider.

The Five Pillars of Islam

Let us turn now to examine the five pillars of Islam which are described in the film. There is, first of all, the act of professing faith. This usually means to assert that there is no god but God and that Muhammad is God's messenger or prophet. That formula in Arabic is called the *kalimah*. The act of profession (*shahada*) is an active disposition. It involves not just adhering with the mind but professing with the lip and believing in the heart. To testify that God is one means to affirm there is only one single, majestic sovereign power that creates, decrees and judges. This one God has revealed himself in a prophetic succession through the ages which culminates in his final and definitive disclosure to the prophet Muhammad. We will return below to the doctrine of revelation which is implicit in the profession of faith.

The second obligation is prayer. This means private, internal prayer, but also communal, ritual prayer such as we viewed in the village mosque. Five times a day the *muezzin* gives the call to prayer; at dawn, at midday, mid-afternoon, sunset and then at the end of the day. At these five junctures of the day, the devotees are summoned to gather for an act of communal prayer. This does not mean that this is the only time to pray, but the devotees are exhorted to pray communally following a sequence of ritual prostrations, some of which we saw.

The strictness with which the duty of prayer is observed varies from country to country, from person to person, and from urban to village and rural regions, and so on. I have seen a traffic policeman in Afghanistan get off the little dias from which he had been directing traffic, and kneel and say his prayers. I have been on buses travelling across Iran and Afghanistan, which have stopped at prayer times enabling the majority of passengers to disembark to say their prayers. They find some water, undergo the necessary ritual ablutions, and attend to their prayers. And yet I have been in mosques at prayer time with very sparse prayer congregations. But it is an obligation that one should, if possible, attend the communal prayer.

The third pillar is the practice of fasting. During the month of Ramadan, the month which com-memorates Muhammad's reception of the first revelation of the Qur'an, devout Muslims fast from the beginning of the day until evening. From the time that a black thread can be distinguished from a white thread at first light, until after the setting of the sun, Muslims are forbidden to drink or eat or take part in sex. Again, this is variously observed. The acids of secularization have penetrated most places in the world and, consequently, fidelity to these traditions has diminished in many centres. Nevertheless, the Ramadan fast is still widely observed.

A non-Muslim in a Muslim country is not required to fast. Although it is probably unwise (as well as insensitive) to be flagrant about eating, it is an obligation which devolves only upon Muslims, though it is not uniformally obeyed. I remember my experience in the Shi'a Muslim area of Baltistan in the Karakoram mountains of northern Kashmir near the Chinese border. Because access to the capital of Skardu requires visual flying below the peaks of the Indian river gorge, it is sometimes necessary to await suitable weather for days or weeks to get in or out. While we were waiting at the airstrip for good weather to fly out of Skardu after our trek to K2, we had a chance to chat for a few days with the young Muslim civil servants of the Pakistan government. It was Ramadan but only some observed the fast. To my astonishment there seemed little censure on the part of those who kept the fast against those who did not. I would have expected, because of stereotypes of Muslim rigidity, particularly in isolated areas, that there would be very strong social coercion, if not internal piety, to motivate observance of the fast. Instead, I detected that this was viewed as a matter of choice. Nevertheless, the tradition does assert a normative obligation to fast during Ramadan and a pious Muslim, whose health permitted, would certainly want to do so. Pregnant and nursing women for whom fasting might be injurious are excused from the obligation, as are the sick and travellers whose journey begins before sunrise.

The fourth pillar is the giving of alms. This is traditionally calculated as a fortieth of one's income (2.5%), though this is debated. Some people say that the taxation system of secular-style governments has supplanted the religious obligation to give alms, whereas others claim that though the government takes taxes a dutiful Muslim must still give alms as a voluntary donation to the poor. The spiritual purpose of this is usually explained as the sensitizing of conscience to the plight of the poor and the needy.

This is not just a social welfare measure; it is a discipline for cultivating a correct moral attitude towards all humankind. The rationale is similar to that given for the observance of the fast. Fasting is justified not simply as obedience to God's undebatable command but as a purposive activity that inculcates sensitivity towards the needy. Muslims understand what it means to be hungry because they have undergone the discipline of not eating or drinking from before sunrise to sunset.

Finally, there is *hajj* or pilgrimage. I have spoken to people who have been on pilgrimages and it seems universally to have been a spiritually edifying and buoyant experience for them. They testify to their sense of the ideal of Islamic brotherhood; of an Islamic community that transcends all racial, national, cultural and economic boundaries. The pilgrims shed their ordinary clothes and wear the prescribed simple white sheet so that the more gross, sartorial symbols of social discrimination are absent. There is a general homogenizing of the pilgrims' appearance and a shared ecstasy with fellow worshippers that encourages them to recognize that every Muslim is a brother to every other Muslim. When they perceive the solidarity of all classes, nationalities and racial colours in the pilgrimage in Mecca, the ideal of

Islamic community — so often violated in ordinary life — receives confirmation as a worthy ideal to be striven for. Moreover, there is something involved in going to a sacred place that does things to human consciousness, that inculcates the proximity of the transcendent.

Let us now consider some other important related terms. At the very beginning of the film we were introduced to the term *qibla* (Arabic for the English word 'direction'). When engaged in ritual prayer, the devotees should face towards Mecca. Specifically, the ritual centre of Islam is the *ka'ba*. This is a squarish building in one corner of which is incorporated a sacred black stone which might be a meteorite. The black stone is surrounded by a silver collar that is replaced from time to time as it becomes worn out by the devotional touching and kissing of the pious. Islamic tradition affirms it to have been there from the beginning when Adam first built the *ka'ba* which was subsequently rebuilt by Abraham and his son Ishmael. This square building is covered at pilgrimage time with enormous black drapes which make it look quite impressive. The *ka'ba*, then, is the geographical centre of Islamic piety towards which the devotees turn during ceremonial prayer. The pilgrimage to Mecca also involves visits to the outlying hill of Arafat where people spend the whole day in prayer in the sun; to the spring of Zamzam where Hagar found water for her son Ishmael when they were dying of thirst in the desert; and to a spot where people throw stones in a symbolic stoning and rejection of the devil. The pilgrimage is something that Muslims are under obligation to perform at least once in their lifetime if their means permit.

Some scholars suggest that the institution of the *ka'ba* illustrates the genius of the prophet Muhammad who, instead of destroying all evidence of pre-Islamic cults, judiciously synthesized some of them into the Islamic vision which he had received by revelation. Instead of extirpating the pre-Islamic lunar cult which had venerated the black stone in Mecca, he assimilated certain external features into the Muslim tradition. This resembles the way Christians incorporated the Germanic celebration of the winter solstice into their Christmas festival, or the way Christians appropriated some of the Jewish holy days, such as Passover and Pentecost, though changing their meanings in the light of their new vision and revelation.

The *qibla* in a mosque is indicated by an architectural device called the *mihrab*. This is a little alcove which indicates the direction of Mecca. Sometimes it is richly worked with mosaic tiles and mirrors, but in a humble village mosque wall it may be scarcely discernible.

It appears that at one point the *qibla*, the direction of prayer, was Jerusalem. When the Jewish tribes in Arabia did not respond to Muhammad's preaching in the manner he expected, God told Muhammad that the direction of prayer was thereafter changed from Jerusalem to Mecca. This is called 'abrogation' in Muslim explanation. In the Qur'anic revelation itself, God has abrogated or retracted some of his earlier decrees. This abrogation, it must be noted, is not something done by man

— Muhammad for example — rather, it is something done by God himself.

Care must be taken in how one interprets this theory of abrogation; it is important to recognize that God foresaw from the beginning of time that Muhammad's proclamation would be rejected by the Jews. Otherwise, one is left with the un-Islamic judgement that the Qur'anic revelation responded to unforeseen, changing historical situations. In the view of most Christians (though not all, certainly not the Baptist fundamentalists portrayed in the film), the Bible reflects the changing historical circumstances of ancient Israel and of the nascent church. The Bible can be analyzed in such a way as to gain insight into the historical circumstances which are seen to be, at least in part, the cause of the Bible being written the way it was. On this view, the Bible reflects the society and culture, the historical epoch, of its composition.

This way of understanding sacred scripture would not be acceptable to orthodox Muslims. For them, the Qur'an does not reflect changing historical circumstances of seventh century Arabia. Rather, the Qur'an is the eternal speech of God. This now needs to be examined more fully.

Muslim Conception of Revelation

To understand Islam one must understand the centrality of the sacred book — the Qur'an — in the consciousness of Muslims. We witnessed the recitation of the Qur'an in Cairo. One would have to be insensitive not to be moved by that recitation whose persuasive power, albeit in a foreign language, could be grasped even by an outsider. It is said that in the recitation of the Qur'an Muslims are moved to tears because of the unparalleled beauty of its language.

The fundamental reason the Qur'an is central to Islam is because it is viewed as the very word of God. Among God's many attributes is that of *kalam*, that is, God's speech. In other words, one of God's intrinsic properties is his communicative capacity. We might call this the expressive character of God. This speech attribute of God is expressed first of all in the Preserved Tablets in heaven. Before there is a Qur'an on earth, there is a prototype in heaven which is called the 'Mother of the Book' because it is the heavenly source of the Qur'an on earth. This divine original is sent down to earth through a process of prophetic revelation (*wahy*), culminating in an Arabic version revealed to the prophet Muhammad over a period of time, beginning in 610 A.D. and lasting for twenty-three years. Because the Qur'an is but an earthly Arabic version of what is written in heaven on the Preserved Tablets, which is itself an expression of God's eternal *kalam* or attribute of expressive speech, the Qur'an is authoritative for Muslim faith and practice. Because it comes directly from the mind of God, the Qur'an possesses an absolute quality.

The following analogy might facilitate an understanding of the status of the Qur'an as the word of God. In Christianity the word of God is Christ. The Gospel of John declares, 'In the beginning was the word, and the word was with God and the word was God. And the word became flesh, and dwelt amongst us, full of grace and truth.' For Christians the eternal word (in Greek: *logos*) is Christ. In Islam the word, the eternal speech of God, is the Qur'an. In both cases we have a communication to earth of an eternal absolute truth. In a structural or formal sense, the concept of revelation is similar, but the substantive way the eternal word manifests itself on earth is very different: a person for Christians, a book (more adequately, enscriptured speech) for Muslims.

We could press that analogy even further. A suggestion has been made by Wilfred Cantwell Smith that the Christian eucharistic ritual of eating the bread and drinking the wine is functionally similar to the Muslim recitation and hearing of the Qur'an. When Christians eat the bread and drink the wine, they are participating in the life of the incarnate Lord. 'Grant us, gracious Lord, so to eat your flesh and drink your blood.' The Christian participates supernaturally in the eternal, divine word through the eucharist. Muslims, through the recitation and hearing of the Qur'an, also participate in the eternal word. The recitation of the Qur'an, one might say, is sacramental, that is, functionally similar to the Christian sacrament of the holy communion.

It is necessary to discuss the connection of the Qur'anic revelation with antecedent revelations because neither the Qur'an nor Muslims claim that this was the only disclosure of God to humans. In fact, the Qur'an takes for granted a prophetic succession. To be a Muslim one must believe in the unity of God, in his angels, in the last day and judgement and — this is crucial for our present purpose — in the books and messengers God has sent. There has been more than one revealed book; there has been more than one messenger from God. There was a prophetic revelation to Adam, to Noah, to Abraham, to Moses, to Jesus, and to a few others who are mentioned in the Qur'an, but not in either the Hebrew or Christian scriptures. It is assumed that God in his kindness, compassion and mercy has sent diverse prophetic witnesses to communicate his will to humankind throughout the passage of the ages.

What has happened in Muslim interpretation is that the recipients of these other revelations — the Jews and the Christians — have lost or corrupted their revelations so that they no longer exist in their normative, pristine form. As Ronald Eyre says, the previous revelations got 'dusted over', which is a charitable way of saying that there has been a per-version of these revealed scriptures! In the seventh century of the Christian era, in Arabia, God sent another revelation to the Prophet Muhammad. This time God's disclosure was in final and complete form. Moreover, this time God took no chances. He guaranteed that in the transmission process there would be no alteration of the revelation. What we have in the Qur'an is what came from God via the mediation of the archangel Gabriel to the Prophet Muhammad.

In fact, the historical evidence seems to be that the Qur'an was quickly enscriptured. Muhammad recited (the name *Qur'an* means recitation) what he had received in his visions or, more accurately, in his auditions. The revelation is basically an auditory phenomenon, not a visual one. These revelatory

pronouncements were committed to memory by disciples and then written down on the shoulder blades
of animals, on palm leaves and on parchment. Very
quickly after his death, the Companions of the
Prophet decided on the canonical Qur'an. The term
canonical means authoritative rule of scripture. The
Companions agreed upon what had truly been
recited by the Prophet and the rest was destroyed.
(In this they may well have been guided by previous
instructions from the Prophet himself.) There was
an unusually rapid passage from Muhammad's reception of the revelation to its being written down.
Muhammad's preaching did not long remain as oral
tradition. More importantly, the process of canoniz-
ing these recitations of Muhammad's was also rapid.
The community of his followers pledged themselves
to the specific body of writings recording his
revelatory auditions as the absolute and normative
regulator of the community's life because of their
origin in the very speech of God. The formation of
the Christian New Testament canon took place over
a longer period of time. The Muslim theological
explanation is that God in his providence, wisdom
and guidance, was ensuring that the revelations to
Muhammad would be transmitted with fidelity to
subsequent generations.

Muhammad as a Prophet
in the Qur'an and in Muslim Piety

Muhammad's status in the Qur'an is that of messenger or prophet of God. He is not a divine being,
not an incarnation. He is a human intermediary
between God and humanity; his role is to receive

God's eternal word of mercy, warning, guidance and judgement to 'recite' it or transmit it to his audience — first in Mecca and, eventually, through his followers, to the world. He is a 'slave to whom it was revealed'.

Unlike Jesus, Muhammad does no miracles except act as bearer of the 'standing miracle' of the Qur'an. He is human with earthly limitations. His uniqueness lies, in the first place, in his having been selected by God to serve as the 'seal of the prophets', that is, the final and perfect spokesman of God's revelation who authenticates all other prophets and claims for truth.

The unadorned portrait of Muhammad in the Qur'an that emphasizes his function as prophet or messenger of God undergoes transformation in the subsequent piety and devotion of Muslims.

In popular piety, Muhammad becomes a miracle worker. He even becomes an intercessor at Doomsday which clearly expands Muhammad's role from that of messenger to that of a sort of salvation figure. He is viewed as completely free of moral defects, totally without sin.

The result of this idealization of the prophet is a profound attention to his personality and to the saving power of his perfect example and mercy. 'Rich and poor, intellectuals and illiterates, have been united in the love of the Prophet, and his presence has been experienced as a continuous blessing' (Annemarie Schimmel). Muhammad becomes an object of devotion and not just a messenger respected for having served as a mouthpiece of God's revelation.

Shari'ah Law

The Qur'an forms the basis of Islamic law. It is frequently observed that theology is not as important in Islamic piety as is law. What God wants principally to reveal to humankind is a straight path, the perfect pattern by which people ought to live. The Qur'an discloses God's straight path, the *shari'ah*. However, as the head of pediatrics at Cairo University pointed out, in addition to the Qur'an as source of law, there is also the *hadith* or traditions. These supply the precedents for behaviour that can be discovered by studying Muhammad's non-Qur'anic words and his practice. The hadith embody the *sunna*, the custom of the Prophet. Muhammad's particular way of doing things was remembered by his followers. When they were subsequently searching for the way the Muslim community should order itself in order to conform to God's will, they called to mind the way the Prophet Muhammad had done things, and this also was regarded as normative. This was justified theologically by the claim that, in addition to having the revelation in the Qur'an, the Prophet also had God-given wisdom, *hikma*, that enabled him to act correctly.

In establishing the body of jurisprudence, *fiqh*, that would structure their community, Muslims also relied on analogical reasoning (*quiyas*). Reasoning is not abjured in Islamic tradition. If a matter is not explicitly covered in the Qur'an or *hadith*, one can nevertheless, by reasoning from similar cases that are treated therein, arrive at legal guidance for the case in question. The final source of Islamic law is *ijma*, or the consensus of the community, though in practice this means the consensus of the early generations of canon lawyers.

This provides an opening to emphasize a point made throughout the film: the centrality of community for Islam. A Muslim friend with whom I studied wrote a book on Christian ethics in which he took exception to what he judged to be Christianity's stress on individual inwardness and subjective piety. With this he contrasted Islam. The glory of Islam, he argued, is that it is a civilization, not just a religion. It seeks not just an inward sense of divine presence, nor just the cultivation of personal morality. Rather, Islam aspires to a total way of life regulated by God's command. This communal aspect of Islam occurs in its emphasis on marriage. It would scandalize most Muslims to hear commonplace western talk such as, 'I don't intend to be married' or 'I intend to be married but I won't have children.' They would object, saying that is not the straight path that God established for human existence. Life lived according to God's ordained structure has to be communal which means, as a presupposition, marriage and children. We observed the signing of the marriage contract which unified the two families, not simply two solitary individuals. The emphasis on law is a confirmation of Islam's resonantly communal outlook.

The dating of the Muslim calendar, to which allusion was made in the film, is significant. The years are calculated from the year 622 A.D. That is neither the birth of Muhammad nor the year when he received his first revelation (which took place in 610). The central date which initiates the Muslim calendar is the *hijra*, sometimes rendered as 'the flight'. The *hijra* commemorates Muhammad's escape from his enemies in Mecca to Medina. Why would an event that, on the surface, looks so ignominious be viewed as the decisive beginning of Islamic history? It is because the *hijra*, as H.A.R. Gibb pointed out, signifies the point at which the Qur'anic revelation became legislation for the community. What had been revealed at Mecca as warning, summons and decree, is now put into practice in Medina. At Medina Muhammad set up a community whose way of life embodied the revelations of God's straight path in the Qur'an.

The very dating of Islamic religious history emphasizes the importance of the community. It is the establishment of an Islamic community submitted to the revealed will of God that is the pivotal point in Islamic history.

Loose ends

I applaud the way Ronald Eyre introduced his last presentation with the 'between you and me' questions. I thought that was an incisive home-spun way of making a good philosophical point that is often made with the conceptual jargon *normative* and *descriptive*. *Normative* pertains to truth; what is really the case about reality and the universe. *Descriptive* is a statement about what people hold to be the case. Whether what they claim to be the case is really objectively true is a normative question which is not easy to answer. It is generally easier (even though that is difficult enough as I believe we discovered) to deal with descriptive questions. For example, what does a devotee in a northern Indian Bihar village really feel about ultimate reality? What is the intention of persons engaged in a Taiwanese shamanistic seance dealing with the question of death? What do they intend to achieve by that ritual? What vision is held of the state of the dead soul?

Normative questions about truth are of this sort: is the soul really being recaptured by those four mediums who, in trance, act out a raid on hell under the supervision of the Taoist priest? Is the soul really recaptured with the assistance of the plague god and restored to some paradisal state, or is that just what the Taiwanese Taoists of that particular sect believe mistakenly to be the case? Between you and me, what is really happening? Is Jesus really the incarnation on earth of the ultimate power of the universe as many people claim? Between you and me, is it really the case that the Buddhist monk, through the process of meditation, develops an intuitive awareness of the real character of existence which is unsullied by ignorant delusions of differentiation. Is there really ultimately only one undifferentiated unity or are there, in fact, discrete things? That is what I mean by normative questions. What is really the case? It is a question of truth.

'Between you and me', normative questions, are not usually the questions with which religion study in a university is comfortable. In a university setting the question — 'Do you really believe in God' meaning 'Is there really a God?'— is not the kind of question typically asked. Neither do we ask, 'Is there really a quality of being represented by the term nirvana?' What we normally ask is, 'Can you describe the Theravada understanding of nirvana?' or 'Can you describe for me the kind of thinking or consciousness that characterizes a person who makes that claim?' The fancy word for that kind of undertaking is 'phenomenological'. We do not push on to ontological questions. We do not press on to say, 'Is nirvana really the way things are?' We simply are content to understand those Buddhist persons who make that kind of claim. In religion study we hold back from these questions of absolute truth.

The questions that Ronald Eyre dealt with at the end in his presentation on *Loose Ends* under the rubric of 'between you and me' fell generally into four main categories. There was, first of all, the question about God. Between you and me, do you really believe in God? There was also the question respecting the function of religion. Between you and me, what does religion really do? Thirdly, there was the question of religious pluralism. Do all religions teach the same thing? Between you and me, is one religion better than the other? That is the problem of religious diversity and religious pluralism. The fourth was the question of the necessity of religion. Between you and me, do you really need a religion to accomplish some of the things that religions allege to do for people? Do you really need that complex, symbolic, creedal, communal, cultic system to deal with questions of death and meaning? Let us look at these 'between you and me' questions.

The Question of God and Language

First of all, the question of God. 'Between you and me,' Ronald Eyre was asked, 'do you yourself believe in God?' Immediately reservations were entered on this question. The first reservation dealt with the frailty and the limitation of language when we engage in talk about God. As Ronald Eyre put it, 'Words have a way of giving out.' We try to explain assertions about Nirvana and the cessation of desire; God, the Father of the Lord Jesus Christ; Yahweh, who bore his people on eagles' wings out of bondage.

Then we find that the language falters, that it seems to be empty, that only people who are within a community of faith seem able to make the mental adjustments that make that language meaningful.

When you say you believe in God, what does God refer to? The first reason the conceptual language I am presently employing is inadequate in talking about God is because, in most religious traditions, God is unique. Our language, particularly our concepts, talk about other things. If there is only one God — if there is no God but God — where shall we find the language appropriate to such a unique being? Is there a special revealed language that allows us to talk about God? We seem, on the contrary, to use ordinary words when we talk about God. If God is unique, how can we use language that is really language about other everyday things to talk about that one unique supernatural being? I could, for example, survey a classroom and say, *young woman, young man, student.* I would be using a language grounded in previous experience. Because I have known a number of young women over the years as students, I can apply such terms to the specific person before me. But if there were only one such person, where would I get my language? The best I could do would be to use her proper name. But, if I attempt to describe a unique being, what kind of language could I use? How can words and meaning about other people or things be made to apply to the one unique individual?

The other related thing is that words have a way of giving out. Words tend to be inadequate when talking about God. God is claimed by religious devotees to be transcendent, that is, beyond our ordinary experience of nature, history, and space-time. Our language has its home-base in mundane things. If I talk about God as shepherd, I am talking in a paradoxical way about the transcendent being who is beyond ordinary experience in terms that are borrowed from everyday life, that is, the life of shepherds. If I say 'God is my king', I am applying to the transcendent being language borrowed from everyday experience — the experience of political authority and monarchy. If one works one's way through all the various images for God, it can be seen that there is a problem of applying to a being alleged to be beyond experience, language which comes from earthly human experience. This immediately raises the question: 'What is the validity of that language; how does it apply?' Theologians and philosophers of language have spent a great deal of time trying to determine exactly what the relation or connection is between language taken from ordinary experience and that applied to a being presumed to be — in important ways — beyond nature and history. For these reasons it is difficult to talk about God. This, then, is the first point: the question of God is difficult because of the inadequacy of human language when discussing God or gods.

God and Transcendence

A second point to be noted is that some confusion might be avoided if we distinguished the terms 'God' and 'transcendence'. If a person is asked 'Do you believe in God?', the natural response is 'It depends on what you mean by God and by *believe*.' This is what Ronald Eyre very wisely said when asked the question. If *God* means a supernatural supreme, personal being, then obviously not everyone believes in God. The Buddhist ultimate, nirvana, is not a personal God, at least not in the Sri Lankan or Theravada Buddhism at which we looked; rather, the sacred ultimate is the ineffable nirvana. A distinction was made between the southern Theravada Buddhism of Sri Lanka and the northern Mahayana Buddhism with its cosmic saviour bodisattvas and Buddhas. In Theravada, or so-called Hinayana Buddhism (at least in its classical forms), the ultimate is not a personal being that can be spoken about in personal terms such as 'shepherd', 'king', 'father', 'mother' or 'judge'. Nirvana is not a personal reality; it is beyond all such predications.

The same sort of judgement might be made respecting Confucianism. There are good grounds for holding that in Confucianism the ultimate social authority is a moral law or pattern, not a personal God who creates, judges and reveals as in Islamic, Jewish or Christian traditions. Similarly, in certain forms of Buddhism the ultimate is conceived as dharma, that is, an absolute, moral pattern. Accordingly, in religious study it is often safer to use a wider term like 'transcendence' to stand for the thrust within all religious traditions to affirm another reality or level of being beyond routine, everyday, profane experience. That other reality, that other truly real level of being, may be a personal God as in Christianity, Islam or the devotional branches of Hinduism, but it may not be. To ask a person 'Do you believe in God?' immediately elicits the counter-response 'It depends on what you mean by *God*.' There are people who believe in nirvana or dharma, as an absolute moral pattern, who do not believe in a personal supreme being.

It is, accordingly, useful to make a distinction between 'God' and 'transcendence'. Transcendence is a wider term which includes personal, supreme being but can also include other impersonal understandings of the ultimate.

Faith and Believing

We said that to the question 'Do you believe in God?' two counter questions are possible: 'What do you mean by *God*?' and 'What do you mean by *believe*?' The answers are not so self-evident as might at first glance appear. Wilfred Cantwell Smith pointed out that when the United Church of Canada appointed a commission to work on a new, up-to-date statement of faith, it examined every word of the Apostle's Creed and the United Church Basis of Union, except the first two words, 'We believe.' They took it for granted that everybody knew what *believing* was. It is not so.

Sister Cecilia, the Romanian nun, thought there was a particular obtuseness, not to say incorrigible sinfulness, about Ronald Eyre; he simply could not believe. Believing seemed to be such a straightforward activity for Sister Cecilia. There is, however, ambiguity about the term *believe*. Bear in mind a distinction which I made before. *Believe* can mean adhering with the mind to certain propositions taken to be true statements about reality. Let us say you are Christian and affirm, 'I believe in God, the almighty Maker of heaven and earth.' By making this statement you are saying *yes* with your mind to the proposition that there really is a supreme personal being who with his power and wisdom made the earth. A Muslim believes, that is, adheres with his mind the proposition, 'There is no God but God and Muhammad is the supreme apostle or messenger of God.' Some religions, like Christianity, have many beliefs and stress the activity of believing. Other religious traditions do not emphasize beliefs and believing as much. Some of the so-called primal religions like the Zulu whose drawings of God were displayed, communicate the reality of God in symbolic images rather than by concepts and doctrines, that is, by beliefs.

In counter-distinction to believing, there is having *faith*, meaning commitment or surrender of oneself with the totality of one's being to what is experienced as supremely true, real, and valuable. There is a profound difference between believing and having faith. Some people, particularly older people steeped in the King James version of the Bible where the language of belief still retains its self-involving tenor, are able to slide from one term to another and to say, 'When I say *believe* I mean *having faith*.' Since 1603 there has been a reinforcement of an intellectualist definition of belief so that *believing* has tended to mean saying *yes* with the mind to certain intellectual statements or propositions which are assumed to be true.

Faith is a different activity than such mental assent, although it may encompass it. Faith is more dynamic in that it is a self-surrendering activity summed up in the word *commitment* to that which is experienced as rightfully authoritative over one's life. When one claims to believe in God is one saying that the odds are — on the available evidence — that the proposition about the existence of a supreme creative spirit or mind is probably true? Surrendering your life, so that all decisions for one's life are made on the basis of this relationship, is a very different kind of activity. Religions are typically concerned to generate this second kind of faith activity. Religions are in the business of generating transformation, conversion, new birth, or radical insight — all terms used by Ronald Eyre. The custodians of a religious heritage are concerned to evoke faith — not the ability to duplicate in a notebook, for instance, the proposition that nirvana means emancipation from ignorance and from samsara, and the dissolution of egoity.

Non-verbal Symbols for God

A further point about the God question concerns the nature and role of non-verbal symbols. Because of the inadequacy of language along the lines just analyzed, non-linguistic symbols become necessary — what the Zulu old man called 'masks' for God. God cannot be seen directly; we see only his masks. We have observed throughout that it is impossible to discuss religion without discussing the symbolic character of religious activity. Because of the sacred's transcendence — the mystery and beyondness of reality — one can only indirectly point to the mysterious transcendent reality through veils. The best veils are probably not the verbal ones. That which cannot be talked about — or can be talked about in only a highly inadequate way — can sometimes be better symbolized by dances and rituals. Most of the religious life that we have witnessed in *The Long Search* has been ritual life. We seem to get closest to what religious people do when we observe their rituals. This is a symbolic activity that makes palpable and accessible to the devotees that which would otherwise be beyond reach. The God who cannot be grasped or perceived in direct vision can be indirectly apprehended through appropriate masks, images, and symbolic acts.

Functions of Religion: Social Cooperation

We turn now to discuss the function of religion. Eyre raised the question, 'What is all of this religious activity for?' It must be admitted that whatever else religion is, it is a very impressive cultural achievement. Our survey of the world's religions has impressed upon us the human insight, energy and discipline, that has gone into the manifold manifestations of religious life. What is it all about? What are religious people doing? Why are they doing it? Is it the opiate of the people as the Marxists claim? Is all of that psychic energy and cultural activity grounded in a monstrous illusion? Is it an ideological means of manipulating and exploiting subservient working classes by projecting their hopes and desires for fulfillment into another realm and another time? One recalls the old quip of religion promising people 'pie in the sky by and by when they die', thus deflecting them from engaging in reform or revolution which will ameliorate the lot of people here on earth.

Ronald Eyre dismisses these reductionist explanations of religion rather quickly. He indicates two functions of religion: first, religion resolves the problem of cooperation. Here in the background is the name of Emile Durkheim (1858-1917) who said that religion functions to integrate people into a moral community. By encouraging people to worship its God, society is really inducing people to worship the community indirectly.

The reason for this, as Durkeim sought to show in his study of totemism, is that the god is really a symbolic representation of the group. When the individuals comprising the group focus on the god, especially in ritual actions, they are drawn together in a powerful fellowship that Durkheim called a church.

It is as if directly exhorting people to revere and respect the authority of the community would not be persuasive. People would very quickly say, 'What right does he or she have to legislate over me?' Religion solves the problem of cooperation among otherwise anarchical individuals by focusing their allegiance on a supreme, transcendent being who simultaneously symbolizes the community and legitimates its social organization and authorizes its social rules. On this social-functional understanding of religion, religion resolves the problem of human relationship or cooperation by integrating the members of society so that they enter into a social contract to abide by the same rules. Religion gives a supernatural sanction for the rules of society.

In many instances, religion inspires attitudes and conduct of love and compassion towards others, especially the poor and rejected. We saw religion undergirding social activity of an altruistic sort in Benares in the practice of Dr. Ashok, who is a novice monk of the Ramakrishna Order. We will refer to the Ramakrishna Order again when we look at the problem of religious pluralism. Dr. Ashok is motivated to serve the people because he feels that in so doing he achieves his own spiritual realization. The supreme reality is in all things. In serving the needs of sick individuals, he is relating himself to that supreme reality, the Brahman, which permeates all things. He could be practising medicine elsewhere, but in the Ramakrishna Hospital there is a special religious atmosphere where the divine spark in every patient is held to the fore. The patients are, for Dr. Ashok, living images of God. This is an instance of religion functioning to generate social concern and service.

I am told that community volunteers in our own society are not so easily recruited now as they were once upon a time. For a number of reasons, everyone wants to be paid now for doing things. Secondly, a lot of the motivation for volunteering one's service came out of an explicit religious commitment. If we are to believe what we read in the papers, religious participation, as measured by church and synogogue attendance, is down to one-third of the population from two-thirds in the 1950s. I began my professional career as a parson at a period of institutional vitality in the 1950s. New churches were being built every second or third month in mushrooming urban areas. Congregations were booming; church programs were vital and numerous. Now things are not that way, except perhaps in some of the fundamentalist churches. What we thought would never happen amongst Catholics has happened; even they are staying away in droves. It may be that the diminution of religious participation also underlies the erosion of the sense of service that used to exist. Certainly one of the functions of religion has been, in one way or another, to establish community; to resolve the problem of how we are to relate to one another; to bring about cooperation, and the cohesive integration of society in place of a collocation of warring individuals.

Functions of Religion: Existential Needs

Another thing that religion does is deal with certain individual needs, often termed 'existential needs'. They might also be called psychological needs. Most prominent among these is the need to deal with the anxiety of death. We met the old mathematician, Dr. Das Gupta, at the Ramakrishna Hospital in Benares who was not sure if he was 87 or 88 years of age. Then we met death in the Taiwanese shamanistic funeral ritual. Ronald Eyre was clearly personally gripped by the role of religion in dealing with death. I suppose that as a middle-aged man, he was beginning to feel his mortality. He was quite sure that secular society could not handle the anxiety of death for him. But death confronts us with a profound human dilemma, threat, and anxiety. Why death? Why do I have to die? Why do my loved ones have to die? Why does death come at such irrational times? I think most of us would settle for a clearly programmed universe in which we all died, between 80 and 110 years of age. But instead death frequently strikes the young mother or father, or child; death is irrational and a source of deep inward dread. Religions help their participants handle the anxiety of death.

The Taoist priest was basically a shaman. A shaman is an intermediary between this ordinary world with its problems, including death, and the spirit world. A shaman can summon spirit helpers to deal with the human problems of death, sickness, hunger and exposure. Another religious functionary was the medium who ritually battered down the gates of hell symbolized by paper towers, then made an inroad into hell and rescued the departed soul for a blissful, heavenly state of life. This sort of ritual activity is one way that religions deal with death.

Ronald Eyre personally felt that secular society cannot effectively handle death anxiety. In fact, secular society typically uses its wealth and energy to try to defeat the demon of death by pretending it is not there. Modernity is busily engaged in the activity of evasion or the denial of death. Religions, on the contrary, confront death because they have a therapeutic answer. They have some kind of solution to the anxiety of death. I found old Dr. Gupta very entrancing. He still admitted to a certain fear of death but he was confident that when death actually came he would be free of anxiety through the power of his religious answer. He said, 'I am an individual, but I shall become universal.' In other words, 'I shall become the all.' When you are part of the *all* there is no longer any individual that can die. As long as you have individuality, you are vulnerable to personal extinction. The all, in contrast, does not die; it is continuous and eternal. Dr. Gupta felt that through the emancipation of spiritual knowledge he would become universal or one with the totality of being. Therefore the fear of death would be abolished.

The third place we saw death was the funeral for the Romanian shepherd. It is very interesting that in the wrap-up of the film Ronald Eyre gives us three clear references to death, obviously testifying to his conviction (and I think it is correct) that religion deals with existential anxieties, individual needs, paramount of which is the anxiety of death, either our own, or the death of loved ones.

Religious Pluralism and Diversity

Another question remains, namely, the question of religious pluralism. It is crystal clear that humankind's religious experience is highly variegated. We have observed many diverse ways in which people are religious. Are all religions the same, or is one better than the other? Eyre introduced some very good climbing sequences as a metaphor for religious diversity and religious truth. He said, 'A religion is instrumental; God is true, not religions. Religions are climbing kits.' To the question 'Is my climbing kit better than yours?' the answer would be 'It depends on what mountain you are climbing.' Ice crampons, essential on snow slopes and ice walls, would be utterly useless on rock faces. Gum friction shoes would serve the rock climber. Eyre's answer, then, to the problem of religious diversity and religious truth would be: 'It depends on what mountain you are climbing.'

I have problems with that answer. My counter-question would be: 'Are we not all basically climbing the same mountain?' Are we human beings not all dealing with the problem of social cooperation? How do we relate to one another? How am I going to get along with my fellows? Is that not a universal problem, endemic to human existence as such? Do not all human beings have to deal with the problem of existential meaning and death? To hold that we are all ultimately climbing the same mountain might entail the conclusion that we should all be using the same basic climbing kit. Even if this point be conceded, it might still be objected that we are not all committed to the same ridge and the same face because of our different historical placement. So, although it might be argued that, in one sense, we are all engaged in the same struggle to liberate ourselves from social strife and the anxiety of meaninglessness, guilt and death, nevertheless, history, fate or God has placed us on different ridges. Hillary climbed Mount Everest in 1953 by the southeast ridge; before long Doug Scott wanted to go up the southwest face. Others sought out the west ridge, and Reinhold Messner did a solo climb without oxygen on the north Tibetan side. History, God, and faith places people on different ridges and on different faces. There we have to choose the appropriate kit.

It may be that one reason why religions generally do not transplant successfully is because they arose, were nurtured, and achieved particular forms in particular geographical, historical, cultural, and social contexts. Therefore they have a peculiar adaptation to those generative conditions. It may be that in a particular cultural situation Hinduism transcends death. In another, European Christianity does. In another context, maybe Tibetan Buddhism may transcend death and create human community more adequately than other, imported traditions would in that same milieu.

It seemed that, at one level, Ronald Eyre did not want to make exclusive truth claims for any one tradition, did not want to imply supremacy for any specific tradition. His judgement appears relativistic: there are different climbing kits for different historical and cultural situations. A relatively modern thinker, Ernst Troeltsch, coined the phrase (which at first glance seems an ambiguity or contradiction) 'relative absoluteness'. This means that in different situations the particular form of religion that people have is absolute for them, but it is absolute relative to those circumstances. So, Christianity is absolute for most people in western culture. Islam is absolute for people in certain lands going from the Atlantic to Indonesia, because in those particular circumstances there has evolved a particular suitability or adaptation of the tradition to that culture. It is absolute for them but not for everyone; therefore, there is relative absoluteness. That is the position that Ronald Eyre espoused.

However, to leap ahead, I think that Ronald Eyre took a personal religious position himself. I do not think there is much doubt that Zen Buddhism was what personally turned him on. That is the climbing kit he was going to choose. Look at the language that betrays uniquely Zen insights and recommendations: 'being there', 'to develop original awareness.' This Zen mode of consciousness is contrasted with our normal way of experiencing the world through conceptual filters. I do not, for example, really see most of my students; I do not know who they are. They are filtered through the conceptual category of 'student'. Each individual is perceived as one of the large group of students enrolled in this course who keeps the Religion Department's enrollment up, maintains our jobs and ensures institutional stability. To be more positive, they are one of the group engaged in this long search to understand religious phenomena. Alternatively, and more concretely, you are a school teacher who needs a credit to get an increase in pay or a promotion. But in every case, whether the category is teacher or student, reality is being passed through a conceptual filter.

Zen, on the other hand, advocates 'being there', being fully aware of everything that is going on. It is a typically Zen experience to focus on the depth latent in ordinary things. We ordinarily, in our profane perception, do not see things as they really are. We usually see them in a utilitarian mode. But if we achieve awakening, if we attain insight, then we can see things as they really are. You are not just a student of mine. The teapot is not just something for brewing an invigorating beverage. It has a depth in itself. That is why Zen stresses the simple things. The bird perched on the bullrush becomes pregnant with transcendental meaning. Ronald Eyre may not have made supremacy claims for Zen Buddhism, but

I do not think there is much doubt that in this smorgasbord of religions he said, 'I am going to choose the Zen climbing kit for the time being.'

I am not saying that you cannot make certain value judgements among or between religions. My own view is that Eyre has got it right. I espouse Troeltsch's view of relative absoluteness of religions which postulates that what a religious symbol systems does for its devotees, another symbol system does for its respective devotees in a different cultural situation. Exclusive truth claims are not only intellectually wrong; they are morally offensive. I am not, however, saying that at certain points you are not obliged to make choices. This is particularly the case with the emergence of many pseudo-religions, or religious symbol systems of a different form such as soccer. Soccer can become demonically idolatrous. You have seen what it does; it has generated a cult of violence among a certain group of people, particularly in the United Kingdom. They live for that weekend excursion where they become someone, where they get a sense of meaning, purpose and mission by their participation in their particular soccer rituals. There is a kind of gnosticism, a kind of conflict dualism between our side and their side. We are on the side of righteousness and are empowered to destroy the powers of wickedness — the other team and its supporters!

Lest you run the risk of becoming excessively tolerant, I would like to remind you of the preeminently, unconditionally perverse, idolatrous and demonic structure of religion in our time, Nazism. Dedication to the world view and value system of the Nazi tradition and participation in its rituals generated a destructive consciousness and commitment. The archetypal symbol of this is the holocaust. Accordingly, distinctions have to be made among religious symbol systems and the kind of selfhood or faith that they create. The kinds of religions we looked at, however, are for the most part universally valuable, true and useful. One must, however, always leave open the possibility of bad religion. That leads me to my concluding point about religion.

Are Religions Necessary?

Do we need religion to solve the problem of social cooperation and the human dilemma of a meaningful, coherent life? Do we need religion to deal with the anxiety of death? Maybe some people can do it on their own; there may be loners who do not need a symbol system. The experience of humankind, for the most part, has been that we cannot do it ourselves. Most people need to participate in a symbol system, a cultural world, that is given to them by God or by society, in order to deal with those human problems of meaning and mortality. We have to leave open the possibility of persons transforming their lives from plight to victory, from chaos to cosmos, from guilt to forgiveness, from death to immortality, from anarchy to love, on their own. The fact is, for most people, this has been achieved through participation in a religious symbol system.

If it were not for that lamentable disease of religions that wants to press on to make exclusive truth claims, then we could say good things about religion almost without condition. But most religions want to press on to say simply, 'We are right; everybody else is wrong, or, at best, only partially right.' Because of this exclusiveness, which is not only a theological error but a moral error, religious traditions also have a dark side. I have, however, stressed for the most part, the human, transformative, positive side of religion.

There are various ways of dealing with the dark negative side of religion such as religious wars, the suppression of conscience and the torture of dissidents. One may be called the normative descriptive cop-out. Whenever these apologists for religion see something bad being done by people who call themselves religious they say, 'That is not really religious.' When Hindu or Muslim mobs attack one another, they say, 'That is not really Hindu or Islam. That is a perversion or deviation.' This raises the question of where the real thing is to be found if not in the hearts and lives of its practitioners. Although there might be some legitimacy to that argument, care must be taken that it does not become an evasion so that whenever religious people do something wicked, the defence is to say that that is not Christian, Jewish or Muslim, although the same advocates are quick to give the credit for good deeds to religious inspiration.

A satisfactory answer to this problem may be to recognize that religion is a human cultural achievement and, as such, is ambivalent. I know of no human accomplishment that is not dialectical, that is, simultaneously evoking a *yes* and a *no*. Religion is typically good and bad at the same time. While religion can deal with the problem of the meaning of existence, it can also become an instrument of self glorification and exclusion. Although Sister Cecilia may have been very saintly, I thought I could detect overtones of smugness and censoriousness towards Ronald Eyre. Both qualities existed at the same time. There are very few unalloyed saints. Religious symbol systems do create meaning in an incoherent universe for their devotees. The messages and mediated realities of religious symbol systems do deal therapeutically with the death of a shepherd in Romania, or of an old mother in Taiwan, or the death anxiety of an old Indian man reaching the end of his span of days. Religions do legitimate social order and inspire responsibility towards others. Christian missionaries, for example, built hospitals and schools. Many, if not most, of the revolutionary leaders in the Third World — certainly in the early phases of decolonization — received their education in Christian missionary schools. There they read the books that convinced them that there is nothing natural or inevitable about colonialism, imperialism or exploitation. Christianity has made positive humane contributions but, at the same time, it has been an instrument — often unwitting — of deculturation and imperial domination.

Call to mind the phrase used to characterize Protestantism — *Ecclesia reformata et semper reformandum* — that is, a church that is reformed and yet is always in the process of reforming. Sister Cecilia of the Romanian Orthodox Church said something similar. Eyre asked her, 'Can a person ever say that they have finally got the truth?' She replied, 'No. No Christian can ever say that.'

A Christian is always in the process of internal reform, of seeking to conform actual practice with ideal profession. I believe this is true of most religions. Islamic fundamentalism is an attempt to reform Islam internally. Some would claim that this reformation has to be reformed itself. When a religious regime starts isolating, jailing and killing Bahai's, that is fundamentalism run amok; it has become demonic, exclusive, destructive.

In this regard, religious activity is similar to all human activity. Parents can be loving and sacrificial yet, at the same time, domineering and destructive. For the same person, the same child, and the same institutional relationship, both things go on at the same time. Religious persons must try to eliminate or diminish the destructive elements in order to assert the humanizing, meaning-giving, death-transcending possibilities of their religious symbol systems.

Printed by
Ateliers Graphiques Marc Veilleux Inc.
Cap-Saint-Ignace Qué.
in April 1991